الفقه الحياة

The Living Fiqh

Workbook One – Purification

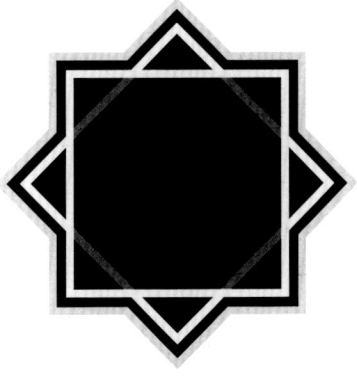

Compiled, translated and illustrated under the guidance of

Ash-Shaikh Sahibzada Muhammad Habib-Ur-Rahman Al-Mahboobi

by M N Sialvi & H B Sahibzada

Published by STI School Publishing
154-156 Sunbridge Road
Bradford BD1 2HA, UK
www.suffa-tul-islam.org

Al-Fiqh Al-Hayaat The Living Fiqh
Workbook One Kitaab At-Tahaarah
© 2009 STI School Publishing

All rights reserved
No part of this publication may be reproduced, stored in a retrieval system, or transmitted in any form or by any means, electronic, mechanical, photocopying, recording or otherwise, without the prior permission of the publisher.

Printed in India

ISBN 978 0 9561397 0 2

Al-Fiqh Al-Hayaat
The Living Fiqh

A NOTE ABOUT THE TITLE

'Al-Fiqh' means 'The Fiqh', by this we are referring to that subject, or branch of Islamic knowledge which covers the understanding of the rulings of Shari'ah. 'Al-Hayaat' means 'The Living,' and together these two words are a noun and adjective sentence meaning 'The Living Fiqh.'

This book has been named 'Al-Fiqh Al-Hayaat' for several reasons:

Firstly it is to give the text a spiritual and intellectual link with the institution of Hayaat-ul-'Uloom Suffa tul Islam, which was founded by the great spiritual teacher and guide Khwaaja Haafidh Muhammad Hayaat Sahib of Dhangrot, Pakistan, may Allah grant him mercy and a place in the gardens of Firdaws with the chosen ones. He laid the foundations for this fountain from which so many, including the authors of this work, are quenching their thirst for knowledge today.

Secondly, the word 'Hayaat' has been translated to mean 'Living', for Fiqh is a practical and 'living' subject which covers every aspect of our daily lives. Our living in this world is based on the rulings of Fiqh which are derived from our Holy Book, the Holy Qur'an and the Sunnah of our Beloved Prophet ﷺ. Every rule and command which makes up the subject of Fiqh is taken from these two main sources, even if it is made by a scholar who has the knowledge and capability to make this ruling. And so, as our lives develop further and the issues which surround us become more complex, it is necessary to have a 'living' subject which will not decay and leave us with unsolved problems in our every-day dealings.

Another reason for naming it thus, is that this text is based on a classic manual of Hanafi fiqh. Indeed it was the remarkable intelligence of Imam A'dham Abu Hanifah ؓ and his tireless pursuit of providing the Ummah of Rasoolullah with an accessible route to perfecting their understanding of the blessed Shariah which makes Hanafi fiqh the most widespread madh-hab (way), from amongst the four madhaahib in fiqh and so it is the most 'living' fiqh throughout the world. [See Appendix A]

بسم اللہ الرحمٰن الرحیم

الحمد للہ رب العالمین، والصلوٰۃ والسلام علیٰ سید المرسلین، وعلیٰ آلہ وصحبہ اجمعین۔ اما بعد، قال رسول اللہ ﷺ: من یرد اللہ بہ خیرا یفقہہ فی الدین۔ الحدیث۔ اللہ تبارک و تعالیٰ جس کو خیر سے نوازنا چاہتا ہے، تو اسے دین کی فقاہت (سمجھ) عطا فرماتا ہے۔

نام کتاب: الفقہ الحیوۃ

وضاحت: فقہ کا مفہوم تقریباً بر طالبعلم سمجھتا ہے۔ الحیوۃ: عربی لفظ ہے، اور یہ مصدر ہے۔ اس کا معنی ہے "زندہ رہنا" (مصدر بمعنی اسم فاعل بھی استعمال ہوتا ہے) (الفقہ الحیوۃ) کا لفظی ترجمہ ہوا (زندہ رہنے والی فقہ) مزید یہ کہ، الحیوۃ سے ایک عظیم المرتبت ہستی کے نام سے منسوب کرنا بھی مقصود ہے، یعنی راقم الحروف کے جدّ ثانی حضرت الاعلیٰ قبلہ عالم حافظ محمد حیات رحمہ اللہ تعالیٰ المعروف حضرت حافظ جی صاحب لنگروٹ شریف والے۔

مؤلف کتاب: حمید نوید سیالوی

آپ کے والد گرامی مشہور زمانہ شخصیت تھے (استاذ العلماء علامہ لبیر احمد صاحب سیالوی رحمہ اللہ) عزیزم مؤلف حضرت علامہ سیالوی رحمہ اللہ کی شہادت کے بعد حیاۃ العلوم صفۃ الاسلام بریلوی فورٹ میں درس نظامی کے سال چہارم میں داخل لیا۔ اور اس وقت وہ سال پنجم کے طالبعلم ہیں۔

عزیزم مولینا نوید سیالوی حصول تعلیم کے ساتھ ساتھ STA کے انچارج اور قابل فخر اساتذہ میں سے ہیں۔ STA ، جدّ و متی اسکول ہے جو صفۃ الاسلام کے زیر انتظام چل رہا ہے۔ اسکول کے نظام اور نصاب میں عزیزم نوید صاحب کی ذہانت کا بھرپور دخل ہے۔ اللہم زد فزد۔

عزیزم نوید سیالوی انتہائی محنتی، ذہین اور صالح نوجوان ہیں۔ ایک با وفا اور باکردار باپ کے با وفا اور باکردار بیٹے ہیں۔ دعا ہے کہ اللہ الکریم میرے اس عزیز بیٹے (علمی نسبتی) کی محنت قبول فرمائے۔ اور انہیں روزافزوں ترقی عطا فرمائے۔ بجاہ سید المرسلین ﷺ۔

نوٹ: عزیز مؤلف نے اس کتاب کا میرے نام سے شائع کرنے کی خواہش کا اظہار کیا۔ جیسے فقیر نے خوشی قبول کر لیا۔ اللہ کریم لعبدہ المجبوب کرم ﷺ وسلم ان کی اس تالیف کو مقبولیت بخشے اور اس میں حبت و عقیدت کو لازوال بنا دے۔ آمین بجاہ نبیہ الامین۔ صلی اللہ علیہ وآلہ وسلم۔

دارلنشر: خویدم الخلق، طوبیٰ لہ الحنی
حمد حبیب الرحمٰن عفا اللہ المنان

CONTENTS

Foreword		1
Introduction		3
Lesson 1	Classification of Water	5
Lesson 2	Types of Water	7
Lesson 3	*Taahir, Ghair-Mutahhir* Water	8
Lesson 4	Leftover Water	11
Lesson 5	Vessels and Wells	13
Lesson 6	*Istinjaa*	16
Lesson 7	Method of *Istinjaa*	17
Lesson 8	*Makroohaat* of *Istinjaa*	18
Lesson 9	*Wudhu*; Introduction & *Fara'idh*	21
Lesson 10	*Wajibaat* of *Wudhu*	24
Lesson 11	*Sunan* of *Wudhu*	25
Lesson 12	*Aadaab* & *Makroohaat* of *Wudhu*	27
Lesson 13	Types of *Wudhu*	29
Lesson 14	What Breaks *Wudhu*	31
Lesson 15	What Doesn't Break *Wudhu*	32
Lesson 16	What Makes *Ghusl Fardh*	33
Lesson 17	What Doesn't Make *Ghusl Fardh*	34
Lesson 18	The *Fara'idh* of *Ghusl*	36
Lesson 19	The *Sunan* of *Ghusl*	38
Lesson 20	*Aadaab* & Occasions for *Ghusl*	39
Lesson 21	*Tayammum*; Introduction & Background	41
Lesson 22	Conditions and Pillars of *Tayammum*	44
Lesson 23	*Sunan* of *Tayammm*	47
Lesson 24	*Mas'h* on Leather Socks	50
Lesson 25	*Mas'h* on Bandages	53
Lesson 26	*Haidh, Nifaas* & *Istihaadhah*; Definition	54
Lesson 27	Effects of *Haidh, Nifaas* & *Istihaadhah*	56
Lesson 28	Types of Impurity	61
Lesson 29	Removal of Impurity	63
Lesson 30	Purity of Hide and Bone	66
Lesson 31	Personal Hygiene, Health & Beauty	69
End Word		74
Appendix A		75
Appendix B		77
Glossary		78

PLEASE NOTE
Answer sheets for all exercises and examination papers (including mock exam papers) are available from the publisher upon request.

STI School Publishing
154-156 Sunbridge Road
Bradford BD1 2HA, UK
+44 (0)1274 732 497
+44 (0)7894 499 189
www.suffa-tul-islam.org

FOREWORD

I begin with the name of Allah the Most Kind, the Ever Merciful

All praise is for the Lord of the worlds who created humans with the faculty of intelligence and understanding. And then He chose our Beloved Prophet ﷺ from the human beings as the model of perfection in understanding and action to deliver the message of Islam.

The book which you hold in your hand has been taken from a very old manuscript written in the 10th year of Hijrah, or the 17th century according to the Gregorian years. The author was called Ash-Shaikh Hasan, the son of 'Ammaar, the son of 'Ali, Abu Al-Ikhlaas, Al-Hanafi, Al-Wafaai, Shurunbulali. He was born in 994 AH in a town on the outskirts of Cairo, in Egypt. He moved to Cairo, to study in the University of Al-Azhar where he was taught and mentored by some great scholars and shaikhs of the time. As a result he also became one of the most famous and renowned scholars of the time. The Shaikh passed away in the year 1069 AH when he was 75 years old. One of his most famous books on Hanafi Fiqh is called **Noor Al-Eedhaah**.

The book you are holding began as a direct translation of **Noor Al-Eedhaah**, however as it was being taught in the first year, it became apparent that this style of direct translation is not understood easily by the youth of the day. And so what resulted was a series of lessons re-written with suitable activities, tasks and additional information to enhance the original script. The order of the lessons, topics, and the detail of the issues is almost exactly the same as in the original text.

This book not only incorporates the issues of Fiqh, but it also touches on wider issues of concern to Muslims and humans in general. It is a very accessible and easy text to understand and teach, furthermore, it uses highly relevant activities to engage the students with the text so that it is not just written words which need to be memorised but a practical way of looking at the issues we face in our daily lives. The book captures the essence of the true meaning of Fiqh, which is to understand- and then it also allows the students to explore practical aspects of the topics at hand and also the wider implications which Fiqh as a subject has in modern times.

This book may be used in conjunction with an original manuscript of the original Arabic text by the teacher to gain a deeper understanding of all the issues. On the other hand it is also possible to teach it as a text in its own right, since all difficult concepts are explained in considerable detail throughout in the form of footnotes.

May Allah ﷻ through His eternal grace and mercy guide the Muslim youth through this sincere endeavour and envelope the author in His special hold, and include him in the ranks of the chosen ones of the Prophets, the Siddiqeen, the Martyrs and the Pious ones. Aameen.

H B Sahibzada, Monday 6th Shawwal 1429 (6th October 2008)

Kitaab At-Tahaarah
Introduction

DEFINITION

The literal meaning of *fiqh* is **to understand**.

Many people have tried to define the knowledge of *fiqh* and several definitions are commonly used. One of the simplest explanations was given by The Great *Imam, Imam Abu Hanifah* ﷺ:

$$\text{مَعْرِفَةُ النَّفْسِ مَا لَهَا وَ مَا عَلَيْهَا}$$

"*The knowledge of your rights and obligations[1].*"

SUBJECT

Fiqh covers a wide area of topics. It includes everything from the birth of a child until the burial of a dead body and even beyond such as inheritance laws. Every aspect of the life of a Muslim is related to *fiqh*.

PURPOSE

By studying the knowledge of *fiqh* a person is able to tell the difference between right and wrong, *halal* and *haram*, and understand his rights and obligations[2], so he can live as a true Muslim.
Fiqh is a practical subject, which requires a Muslim to act upon it. It sets out the guidelines of how a Muslim should live in this world. Following these guidelines will ensure a better life in the hereafter.

THE SOURCES OF FIQH

Fiqh is taken from four sources. They are:
1. The Holy *Qur'an*,
2. The *sunnah* of *Rasoolullah* ﷺ,
3. The agreement of the scholars (consensus),
4. *Qiyaas* (logical comparison).

In order to find the answer to a particular problem, we would first turn to The Holy *Qur'an*, then the *ahadith* of *Rasoolullah* ﷺ, then what the scholars have agreed on. If it is still not resolved then a qualified scholar would use his intellect to come to a ruling based on the *Qur'an* and the *sunnah*. [See Appendix B]

---

[1] مرآة الاصول (Mir'aat Al-Usul), التوضيح لمتن التنقيح (At-Tawdeeh Limatn At-Tanqeeh)

[2] حقوق الله و حقوق العباد The rights of Allah ﷺ and the rights of fellow humans.

THE IMPORTANCE OF STUDYING *FIQH*

The importance of *fiqh* can be seen from the following *hadith* of *Rasoolullah* ﷺ:

مَن يُرِدِ اللهُ بِهِ خَيْراً يُفَقِّهْهُ فِى الدِّيْنِ

"Allah gives an understanding of Islam to whoever he intends well for."
[Bukhari & Muslim]

From this *hadith* we learn that from amongst His people, *Allah* ﷻ selects certain people for whom He has a good ending prepared. The first sign of this is that He makes them a part of the *ummah* of *Rasoolullah* ﷺ. The second sign is that *Allah* ﷻ selects them from amongst this *ummah* for learning and understanding the knowledge of Islam.

In another *hadith* the Messenger of *Allah* ﷺ said that the angels spread their wings for a student when he leaves his home in search of knowledge. All the creatures, even the ants in their burrows and the fish in the sea pray for him until he returns home.

Indeed those lucky individuals who have been chosen to be enveloped in the wings of angels should be grateful for this great favour upon them from *Allah* ﷻ, the Lord of the worlds.

KITAAB AT-TAHAARAH (The Book of Purity)

Almost all *fiqh* books begin with the chapter of purification. This is because before you can do any form of worship you must be clean and pure. It is also important for all Muslims to remain clean and pure all the time because *Rasoolullah* ﷺ said:

اَلطُّهُوْرُ شَطْرُ الإِيْمَانِ

"Cleanliness is half of faith."
[Muslim]

This *hadith* makes it clear that remaining clean is a part of being a Muslim. Just as a person's faith must remain firmly rooted within his heart all the time, so too must the love of cleanliness. This includes remaining clean physically and spiritually. The different aspects of cleanliness will be discussed in much more detail in this chapter, *insha-Allah*.

Exercise — Memorise the Arabic text of the ahadith mentioned above, together with their meanings.

Lesson 1
Water

THE CLASSIFICATION OF WATER

We will begin by looking at water; its types, whether it is permissible to use, how to purify it if it becomes impure etc; because water is the essential tool for achieving purity.

It is permissible to use seven types[3] of water for the purpose of attaining purity:

1. Rain water,
2. Sea water,
3. River water,
4. Well water,
5. Melted snow,
6. Melted ice,
7. Spring water.

Then water is divided into five types[4]:

1. Taahir[5], mutahhir[6], ghair-makrooh[7],
2. Taahir, mutahhir, makrooh[8],
3. Taahir, ghair-mutahhir[9],
4. Najas[10],
5. Mashkook[11].

> **THINK!**
>
> Life on this planet depends on water. All living creatures, even plants depend on water. We depend on it, so much so that 65% of our bodies are composed of water*. We use it in almost every type of production industry. We would not be able to build these fast cars, long trains, tall skyscrapers... we wouldn't even be able to exist without it. Next time you use water for anything, and every time after that, THANK ALLAH who gave us this amazing blessing by saying **Alhamdulillah!**
> *Encarta Encylopedia

---

[3] These are the seven types of water based on its source, i.e. where it comes from.
[4] These five types of water are based on its purity.
[5] (طاهر) Taahir: It is clean/pure
[6] (مطهِّر) Mutahhir: It cleans/purifies
[7] (غير مكروه) Ghair-makrooh: It is not disliked
[8] (مكروه) Makrooh: Disliked
[9] (غير مطهِّر) Ghair-mutahhir: Does not clean/purify
[10] (نجس) Najas: impure/unclean
[11] (مشكوك) Mashkook: Doubted/uncertain

Exercise – Wordsearch

Find the following words in the grid below:

- Snow
- Najas
- Well
- Taahir
- Ghair Mutahhir
- Sea Water
- Rain
- Makrooh
- Fiqh
- River
- Spring Water
- Ice
- Mashkook

s	e	f	h	o	m	k	o	o	k	h	s	a	m	z	d	e	a	b	j
h	b	z	x	g	f	g	d	s	l	p	n	h	y	i	r	k	l	h	s
t	u	t	a	a	h	i	r	u	i	r	a	q	s	v	t	n	k	q	a
m	v	e	z	a	y	a	y	s	e	a	w	a	t	e	r	t	f	m	j
a	z	s	w	v	b	m	i	r	e	d	g	y	f	a	c	m	h	l	a
h	j	l	a	d	h	t	m	r	j	n	v	x	i	c	a	s	e	t	n
e	v	u	i	n	t	t	a	v	m	v	r	t	q	f	w	e	l	l	y
a	a	h	o	o	r	k	a	m	e	u	e	w	h	t	y	u	i	j	c
p	y	b	r	y	i	o	a	k	l	e	t	o	t	b	m	o	q	o	l
j	d	s	p	a	j	k	z	w	r	e	t	a	w	g	n	i	r	p	s
f	r	n	o	c	n	s	d	d	f	s	w	e	h	e	u	v	s	g	h
n	j	o	m	x	i	k	t	g	h	l	r	m	j	h	n	e	u	f	b
k	a	w	e	t	a	j	g	i	a	e	b	n	l	h	i	g	k	l	a
i	w	t	g	y	r	w	b	i	v	s	b	a	z	a	e	r	q	j	k
z	c	n	g	k	b	r	j	i	q	w	v	a	u	p	u	a	a	g	h
f	c	e	a	j	m	y	r	k	x	c	g	l	q	o	p	h	z	x	a

Lesson 2
Water

THE FIVE TYPES OF WATER

1. *Taahir, Mutahhir and Ghair Makrooh.* It is pure and it purifies and its use is not *makrooh*. This is simply any of the seven types or fresh (unused) water.

2. *Taahir, Mutahhir and Makrooh.* It is pure and it purifies but its use is disliked. An example of this is water that a cat has drank from.

3. *Taahir, Ghair Mutahhir.* It is pure but does not purify. For example, water which has been used to remove *hadath*[12], or has been used to perform *wudhu*[13] with the intention of *thawab*[14]. This type of water will be discussed in more detail in the next lesson, *inshaAllah*.

4. *Najas.* It is not pure; so it does not purify. If water which has a *najasah*[15] mixed in it, is less than ten-by-ten yards and is not flowing it becomes *najas* whether the effect[16] of the dirt is apparent or not. Or it becomes *najas* if the water is flowing and the effect of the *najasah* is present.

5. *Mashkook.* There is doubt in the purity of this type[17]. This is water which a donkey or mule has drank from.

Exercise

Memorise these words and their meanings:
Taahir   Najas
Mutahhir   Mashkook
Makrooh   Hadath

---

[12] (حدث) Hadath is a state of impurity. There are two types of hadath. Al-hadath al-asghar (minor impurity) and al-hadath al-akbar (major impurity). Minor impurity means not being in wudhu. Major impurity means for ghusl to be fardh upon you.

[13] (وضوء) Wudhu. The washing which removes al-hadath al-asghar

[14] (ثواب) Thawab. Reward/blessing

[15] (نجاسة) Najasah: Impurity.

[16] "Effect" means taste, colour or smell.

[17] The doubt is not because the scholars did not know whether it is pure or not but because they had different opinions, some said it is pure, others said it is impure.

Lesson 3
Water

TAAHIR, GHAIR-MUTAHHIR WATER

- Water becomes *musta'mal*[18] as soon as it separates from the body.
- Fruit-juice or any type of plant-juice cannot be used for performing *wudhu*[19].

- If the true state of water has changed it cannot be used. This can happen in two ways:
    1. If the water has been used for cooking (e.g. curry).
    2. If another substance dissolves in the water and changes its thinness or ability to flow.
- If a solid, such as leaves, falls into the water and causes its taste, smell and colour to change it may still be used for *wudhu*. [See Figure 1.1]

- If a liquid mixes with water then there are three possibilities:
    1. If the liquid has three properties (colour, taste, smell) and two of those properties show in the water; you cannot use this water for *wudhu*.
    2. If the liquid has two properties (e.g. milk) and one of these shows in the water, you cannot use it.
    3. If the liquid has no properties, for example used water, then we will look at the proportion of used and unused water. If there is more used water in the mixture then you can't use it for wudhu, otherwise you can. [See Figure 1.2]

Q&A

Answer the following questions in your exercise books:

1. At what point will water be classed as 'used'?
2. Is it permissible to use apple juice to do wudhu?
3. Is it permissible to do wudhu with water that has vinegar mixed in it?
4. Can you do wudhu with unused and used water mixed together?
5. What does it mean when water is 'overcome' by something else?

---

[18] (مستعمَل) Musta'mal. Used
[19] Even if the juice comes out by itself.

Figure 1.1

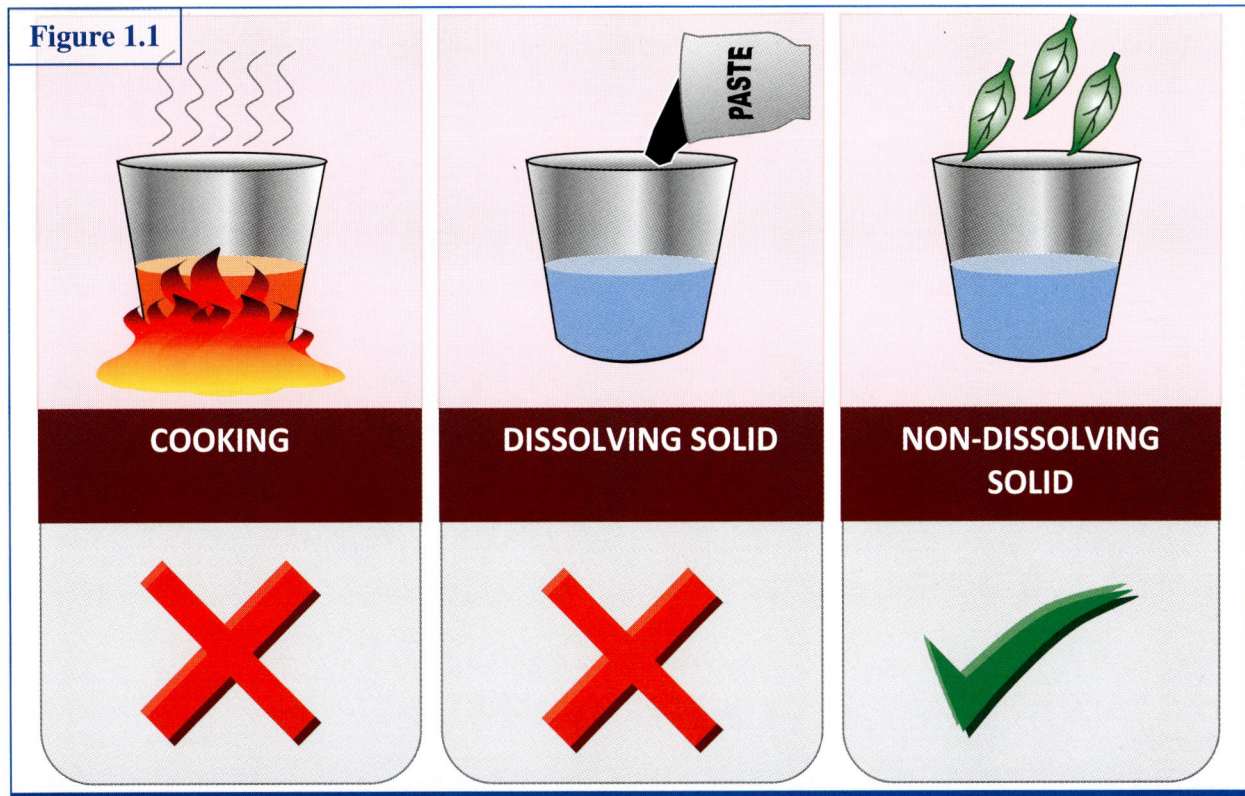

The true state of water can be changed if its fluidity is changed by cooking or if a dissolving solid mixes with it. If this happens it cannot be used for wudhu.

Figure 1.2

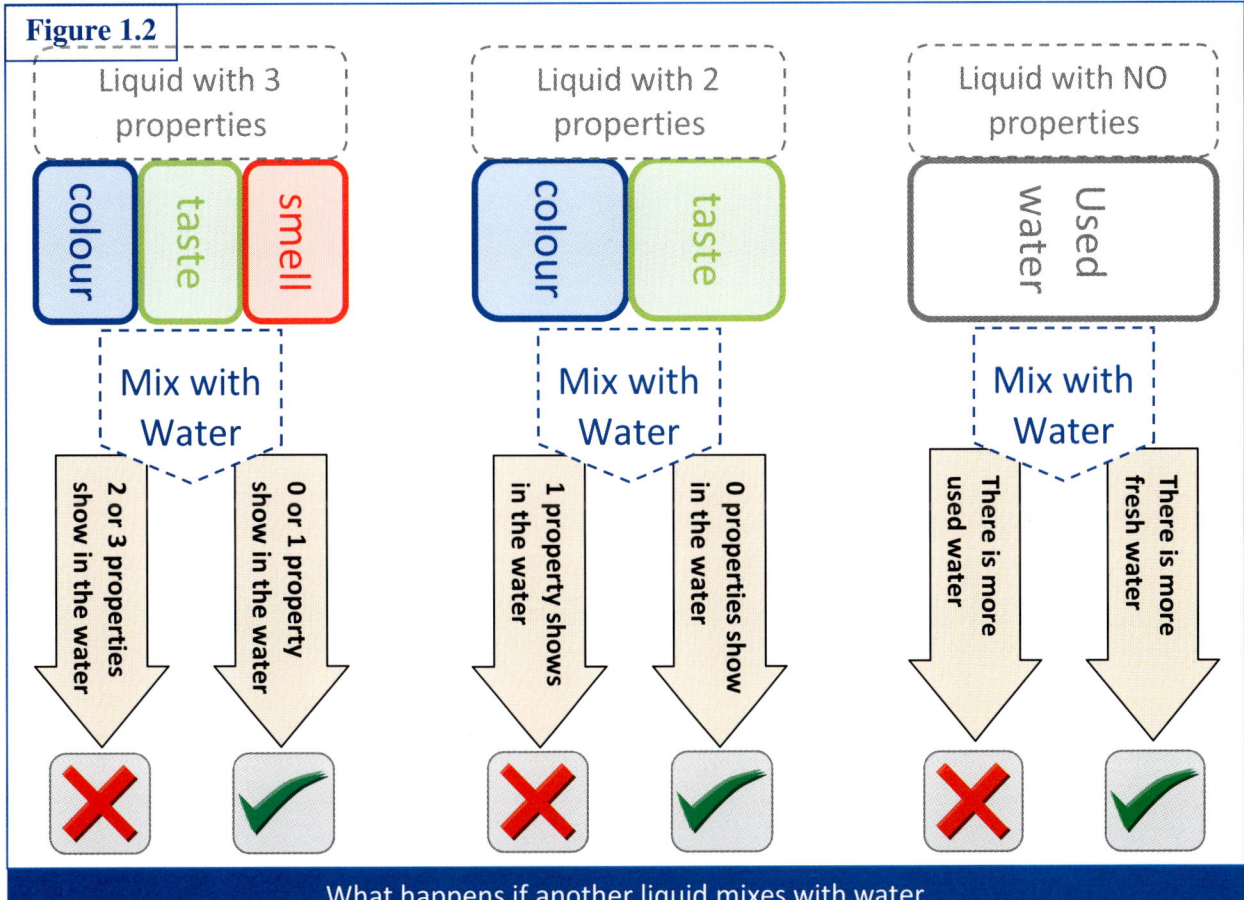

What happens if another liquid mixes with water.

9

USED WATER

UNUSED WATER

1. If the water from bucket H was mixed with the water from bucket D; can wudhu be done with it?

    Y ☐   N ☐

2. If the water from bucket J and bucket B was mixed; can wudhu be done with it?

    Y ☐   N ☐

3. If the water from bucket F and bucket J was mixed together; would it be okay to do wudhu with it?

    Y ☐   N ☐

4. Can the water from bucket E be mixed with bucket I for wudhu?

    Y ☐   N ☐

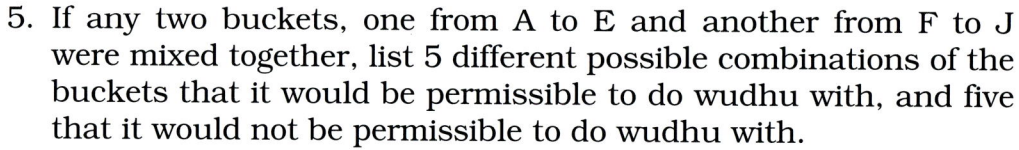

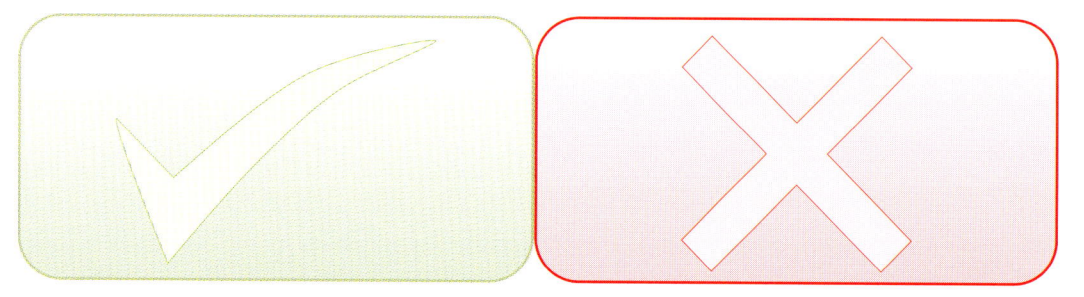

5. If any two buckets, one from A to E and another from F to J were mixed together, list 5 different possible combinations of the buckets that it would be permissible to do wudhu with, and five that it would not be permissible to do wudhu with.

Lesson 4
Water

LEFTOVER WATER

When an animal drinks from a "small amount[20]" of water, the remaining water is called "*soo-r*[21]." *Soo-r* is of four types

1. ***Taahir, Mutahhir.*** It is pure and it purifies. This is that water which a person, a horse or any halal animal has drank from.

2. ***Najas.*** It is not pure so does not purify; its use is not permitted. This is that water which any of the following have drank from:
    - A dog,
    - A swine (includes pig, hog and boar),
    - A predatory animal, such as a cheetah or wolf.

3. ***Makrooh.*** The use of this type is *makrooh* (disliked) when other water is available. This is that water which any of the following has drank from:
    - A cat,
    - A free-range chicken,
    - A bird of prey, such as a kestrel, eagle or buzzard,
    - Small animals that live in houses, such as mice[22].

4. ***Mashkook.*** The purity of this type has been doubted. This is that water which a donkey or mule has drank from. If this is the only water available then you should perform *wudhu* with it then perform *tayammum*[23] before performing *salah*[24].

---

[20] Less than 10×10 yds

[21] (سُؤْرٌ) Soo-r means leftover.

[22] Excluding scorpions.

[23] (تَيَمُّم) Tayammum. Purification without water. See chapter on Tayammum for more detail.

[24] (صلوٰة) Salah. In Fiqh, salah means the five daily prayers which are fardh upon every Muslim, male and female.

PRACTICAL ACTIVITY

The following activity will be carried out in groups of 3-5. Each group has been given 13 plastic cups containing imaginary leftover water. Each cup is labelled with one of the following labels:

a. Person
b. Horse
c. Cow
d. Goat
e. Lion
f. Free-range chicken
g. Scorpion
h. Dog
i. Eagle
j. Cat
k. Mule
l. Wolf
m. Pig

There are 4 tables labelled as follows:
a. Taahir Mutahhir
b. Makrooh
c. Najas
d. Mashkook

When your group is called out by your teacher, you must place the cups on the correct tables to show which category the leftover of each animal belongs to.

Lesson 5
Water

THE PURITY OF CROCKERY & VESSELS

If there is a mixture of containers for storing, carrying or pouring water and most of them are *taahir*, then you should guess and try to choose a *taahir* one for performing *wudhu* with or for drinking from.

If, however, most of the vessels are *najas* then thought and contemplation need only be given when choosing one to drink from.

If there is a mixture of *taahir* and *najas* clothes then you should investigate and try to select a *taahir* one from them, regardless of whether most of them are *taahir* or *najas*.

THE PURITY OF WELLS

If *najasah* falls in to it.
A small well becomes impure, and so all its water must be removed, when any *najasah* falls into it, even if it is a small amount, such as a single drop of blood or alcohol (this excludes dung[25]). It also becomes impure if a pig falls into the well, even if it comes back out alive and its mouth has not reached the water.

If something dies in it.
The death of a dog, goat or person in a well also makes it impure, or if any other animal, small or large, dies in the well and its body swells up from remaining in the water.

If it is not possible to empty the well of all its water[26] then two hundred buckets of water need to be removed from the well in order to purify it.

If a chicken, cat or anything similar dies in the well, then forty buckets of water need to be removed to purify it.

If a mouse or its like dies in the well, then twenty buckets of water need to be removed to purify it.

When the required amount is removed it purifies the well, the rope, the bucket and the hands of those removing the water.

---

[25] The reason why dung is excluded is to create ease for people because it is a common thing for a small amount of dung to fall into a well. If lots of dung is seen in the water then it will be impure.
[26] Not all wells are the same; some wells have an underground stream below them which means that when any amount of water is taken out of the well it is immediately replaced making it impossible to actually empty the well. Other wells have a slower system of filling up and it is possible to remove the water quicker than it is replaced and thereby emptying the well.

When is a well not impure?
A well is not made impure by the following: goat or sheep droppings; horse, donkey or mule manure; cow manure; unless it is seen in a large quantity in the water; or if every bucketful of water removed contains droppings in it.

Water does not become impure by the droppings of small birds such as pigeons and sparrows, nor if any creature dies in it that has no circulating blood in its body, such as fish, frogs and other aquatic creatures, nor a mosquito, fly, bee, or scorpion.

Water is also not made impure if a person or any *halal* animal falls into it and comes back out alive as long as there was no impurity on its body.

According to authentic narrations, water is not made impure if a mule, donkey or any predatory animal falls into it. If the saliva of the animal mixes with the water, then the water will be categorised according to the ruling on the saliva of that animal.

What if it is not known when the water became impure?
When no one knows how long a dead animal has been in the water, it will be considered impure for 24 hours prior to its discovery. If the body of the animal has swollen up, then the water will be deemed impure for 72 hours before the animal was found[27].

Activity

Draw a picture showing a cross-section of a well on a piece of A3 paper, then peel the labels overleaf and stick then in your well. Now fill in the correct number in each bucket to show how many of these buckets need to be removed to purify the well. Lastly peel off the four circular pictures and stick each one next to the bucket with the correct number on it. The key below shows what it means if the outline of the picture is black, grey or dotted.

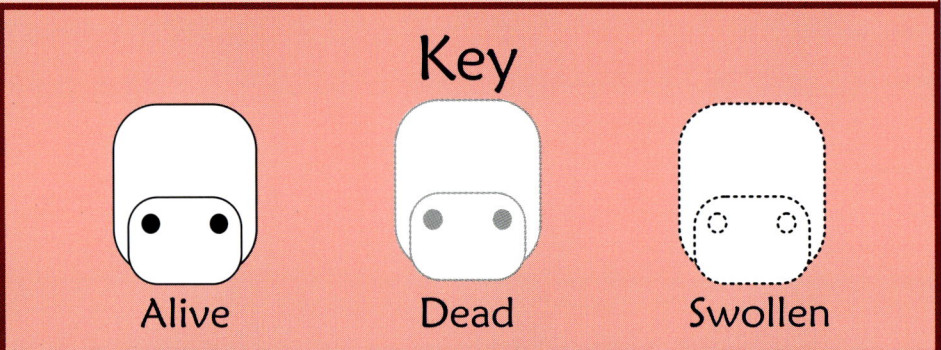

[27] This means that anyone who used this water for wudhu must repeat any prayers he prayed with that wudhu during the previous 24 hours if the animal is dead not swollen, and 72 hours if the animal is swollen.

NOTE: For stickers, see the 'Sticker Section' at the back of this book

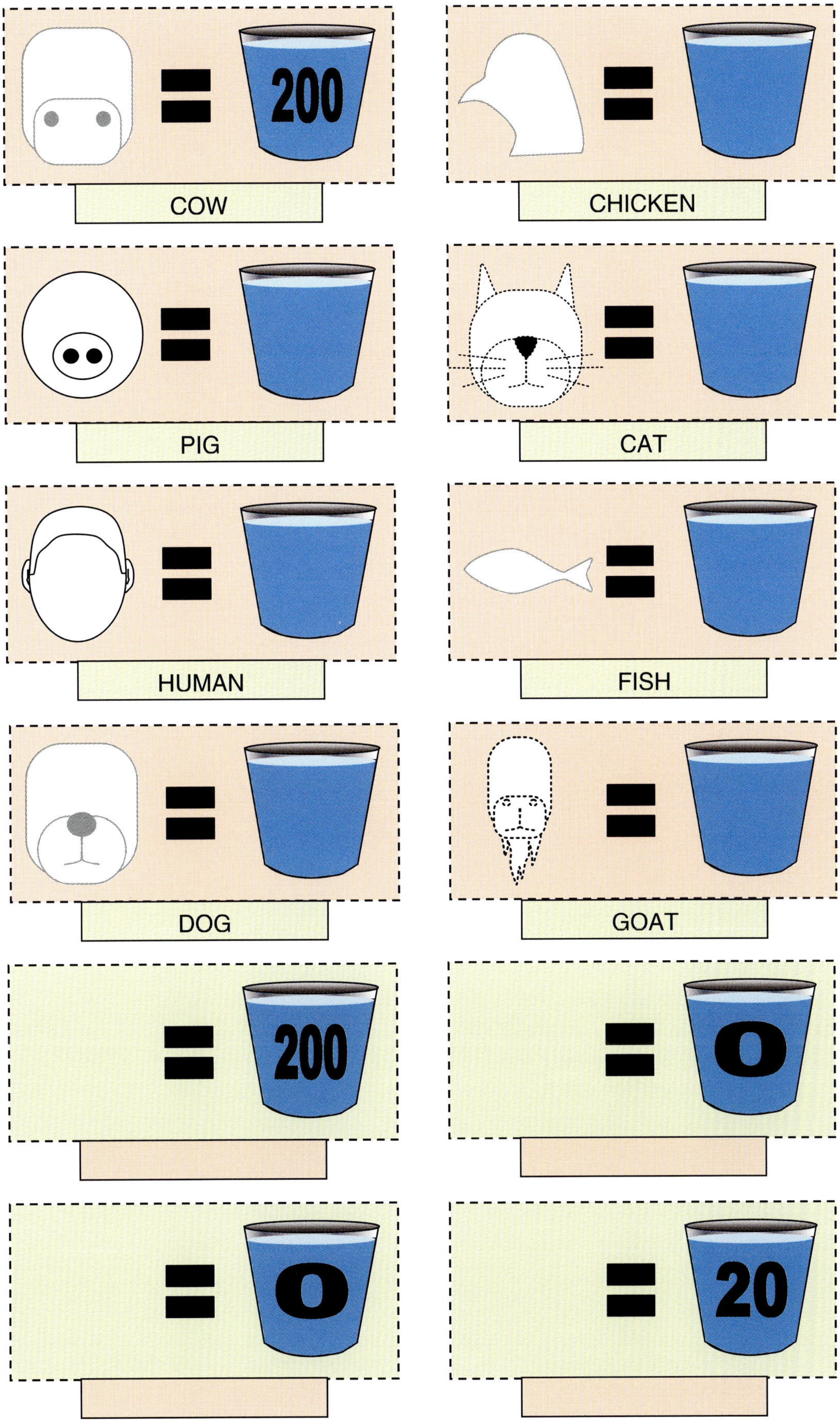

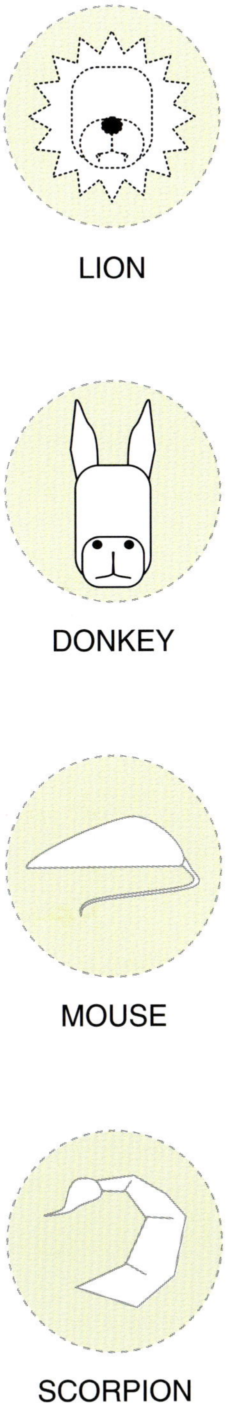

COW = 200	CHICKEN =
PIG =	CAT =
HUMAN =	FISH =
DOG =	GOAT =

= 200   = O

= O   = 20

LION

DONKEY

MOUSE

SCORPION

15

Lesson 6
Istinjaa

A FEW THINGS REGARDING *ISTINJAA*[28]

- A man must be sure that all the drops of urine have finished before he begins to perform *wudhu*.

- *Istinjaa* is *sunnah* when any *najasah* is excreted from either of the two passages[29] and the *najasah* does not spread from its origin.
- If the *najasah* spreads to an area the size of one *dirham*[30] then it is *wajib* to remove it using water.
- If it spreads to an area greater than one *dirham*, it is *fardh* to remove it.

- When bathing after *janabah*[31], *haidh*[32] or *nifaas*[33], it is *fardh* to wash the private parts and to remove anything at and around the private parts, even though the amount of the *najasah* may be very little.
- The purpose of *istinjaa* is to become clean so it can be done using a tissue. Using water is better and using both tissue and water is best.
- To use three tissues is *mustahab*[34].

ALLAH SAYS:

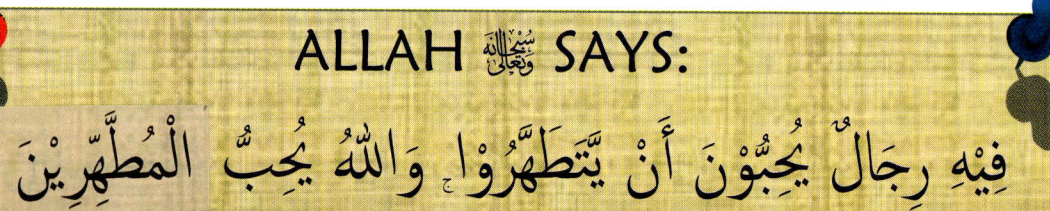

...In this masjid (of Qubaa) there are some people who wish to be well cleansed, indeed Allah loves clean people. [9:108]
When this verse was revealed, our Beloved Prophet ﷺ asked, oh group of Ansaar! Allah has revealed this verse in your praise; what is your practice when you do istinjaa and wudhu?
The Ansaar said that they used three pieces of earth (in place of tissue) before washing with water when doing istinjaa.
[Tafseer Irfan Al-Qur'an – Allama Syed Muhammad Na'eemuddin رحمه الله]

---

[28] (الاستنجاء) The name given to the washing/cleaning of the private parts after going to the toilet.

[29] (سبيلين) Two passages means urinary and excretory tract

[30] approximately a circle of one inch diameter (or 3cm^2)

[31] (جنابة) The state of major impurity

[32] (حيض) The menstruation period

[33] (نفاس) The period of bleeding after childbirth

[34] Mustahab means preferred.

Lesson 7
Istinjaa

HOW TO PERFORM *ISTINJAA*

- A man should begin by wiping from the front towards the back with tissue first, then from the back towards the front and then from the front towards the back.

- Women should always wipe from the front towards the back[35].

- Next the hands should be washed and then the area of impurity should be washed whilst scrubbing.

- Cleanliness should be achieved fully until there is no disliked smell remaining.

- The ruling for someone who is not fasting is that he should relax the backside for thorough cleaning.

- Someone who is fasting should dry the area washed before standing up[36].

- The hands should be washed thoroughly at the end.

THINK...

...Some people see Islam as an out-dated way of life, yet the 'civilised' western world was lost in the darkness of ignorance until recent times. It was common practice amongst the Victorians to throw the contents of their sanitary basins out onto the streets. Bathing was a ritual that only the elite in society performed and only on very special occasions.

On the other hand, Muslims were encouraged to wash five times a day for each salah, and after every time they answered the call of nature hundreds of years before all this was happening in Europe.

---

[35] To ensure that the farj ad-daakhil is not contaminated.
[36] This is to eliminate the chance of any water reaching the stomach through the excretory tract and thus breaking the fast.

Lesson 8
Istinjaa

THE *MAKROOHAAT*[37] OF *ISTINJAA*

a) Undressing the *awrah*[38] for *istinjaa* is not allowed in front of another person.

b) It is *makrooh* to perform *istinjaa* with the following:
   1. A bone,
   2. Human or animal food,
   3. A brick,
   4. A piece of earthenware/pottery,
   5. A piece of coal,
   6. Glass,
   7. Lime (as in limestone),
   8. Any object that is valuable or deserves respect such as expensive silks, writing paper etc.

c) It is also *makrooh* to perform *istinjaa* with the right hand[39].

d) You should enter the bathroom/lavatory with the left foot and recite the following du'a before entering:

اَعُوذُ بِاللهِ مِنَ الشَّيْطَانِ الرَّجِيمِ ۝

A'oozu billahi min ashaytan-ir-rajeem[40]

e) You should NOT speak whilst in the lavatory (unless absolutely necessary).

f) It is *makrooh tahrimi*[41] to sit facing the *Qiblah*[42] or with the back to the *Qiblah* (even in an enclosed/indoor lavatory).

g) It is also *makrooh* to urinate or excrete in water (such as a pool or stream etc[43]), in the shade[44], in a hole[45], on a pathway[46] and under a fruit-bearing tree[47].

---

[37] (مكروهات) Makroohaat: Plural of makrooh, meaning those actions that are disliked.

[38] (عورة) Awrah: The area of the body that is fardh to cover up. For a man this is the area between the naval and the knees, for a woman this is the entire body, except hands, face and feet.

[39] Except with a valid reason.

[40] I seek Allah's protection from Satan, the cursed one.

[41] (المكروه التحريمى) Makrooh tahrimi: Extremely disliked, these actions are close to haram.

There are two types of makrooh: Tanzihi (less disliked) and tahrimi (exteremely disliked). When the word makrooh is mentioned and it is not specified whether it means tahrimi or tanzihi, it usually means tahrimi.

[42] (قبلة) Qiblah. The direction of the Holy Ka'bah.

h) It is *makrooh* to urinate whilst standing.

i) You should exit the lavatory with the right foot and recite the following du'a:

اَلْحَمْدُ لِلّٰهِ الَّذِىْ اَذْهَبَ عَنِّى الْاَذٰى وَ عَافَانِىْ

Alhamdu lillahilladhee adh-haba 'annil adhaa wa 'aafaanee[48]

Memorise... ...the Arabic text of the du'as mentioned above, together with their meanings.

Write... ...the meaning of the word 'makrooh' and its types:
_____
_____
_____
_____
_____

Explain... ...what lessons we can learn from paragraph 'g' regarding the following topics:
good citizenship
animal rights
care of nature
conservation & ecology

---

[43] This is because the pool may be a source of drinking water for animals or people and it would be wrong to contaminate it.

[44] People/travellers use areas of shade to rest and escape the heat of the sun, it is wrong to urinate or excrete in such areas as it causes discomfort to others.

[45] As this hole may be home to an animal, and Islam teaches us that we should protect the rights of animals also, not just people.

[46] It is wrong to excrete or urinate on a pathway as this will be used by people and could contaminate someone's clothes etc.

[47] If the fruit falls off the tree and there is urine or faeces on the ground then the fruit will become contaminated and will not remain edible.

[48] All praise to Allah who took trouble away from me and gave me safety.

CROSSWORD EXERCISE

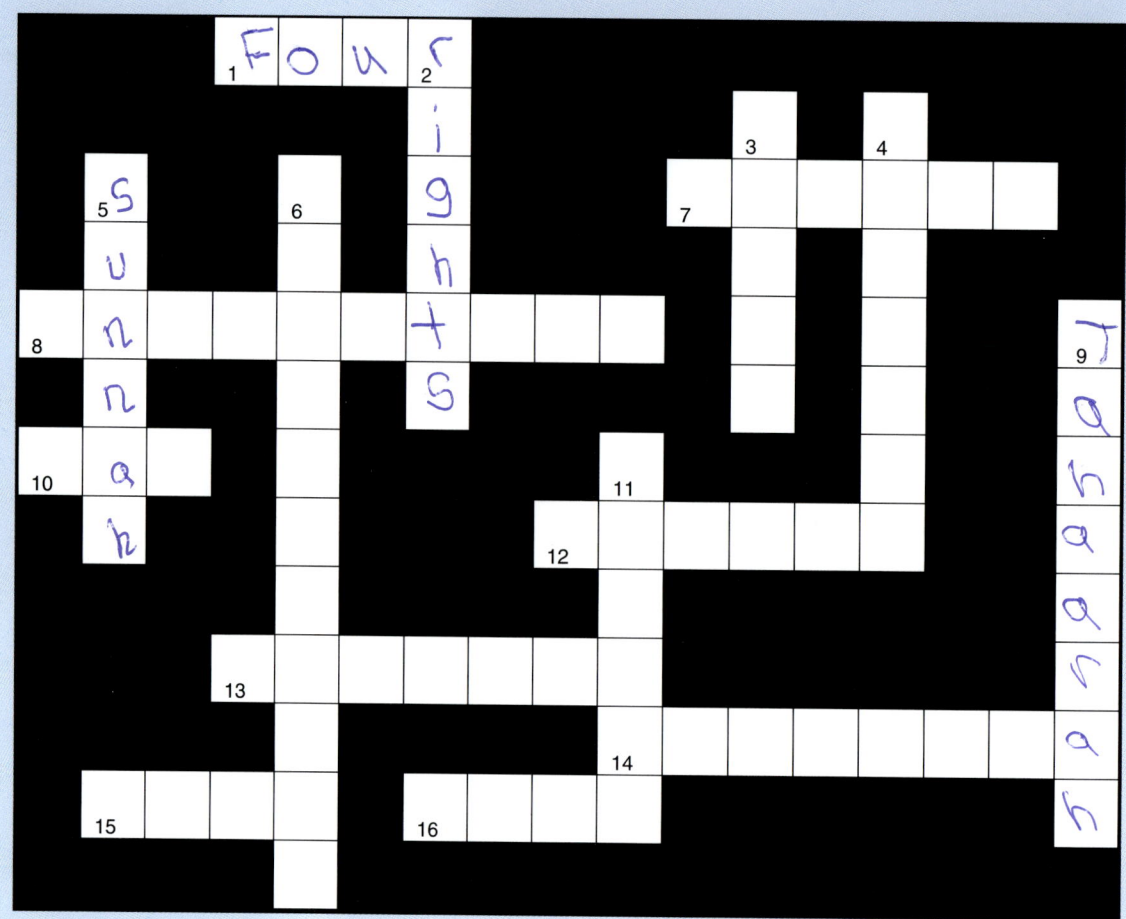

Down
2 Fiqh is to know your ……… and obligations
3 It is makrooh to face this whilst on the toilet
4 Impurity
5 The second source of fiqh
6 A type of taahir mutahhir water which comes from underground through rocks
9 The first chapter in most fiqh books is called "Kitaab At-_____"
11 It is pure

Across
1 The number of sources of fiqh
7 Post-natal bleeding
8 The literal meaning of fiqh
10 Its leftover is makrooh
12 A state of impurity
13 Disliked
14 The name of cleaning the private parts
15 Its leftover is mashkook
16 Leftover

Lesson 9
Wudhu

DEFINITION

Wudhu is the name given to the washing of three parts of the body and the *mas'h* (wiping) of one part. This washing removes *al-hadath al-asghar* (minor impurity).

PURPOSE

The purpose of *wudhu* is so that you are able to do all those things which you are not allowed to do without *wudhu*. This is its purpose in this life and the reason for *wudhu* regarding the next life is *thawab*.

BENEFITS

The following are some of the benefits of *wudhu* which have been mentioned in the *ahadith*:
1. *Wudhu* washes away the sins[49].
2. All the parts washed during *wudhu* will shine brightly on the day of judgement, and those parts will be decorated in paradise[50].
3. *Wudhu* helps you to develop the habit of keeping clean[51].

CONDITIONS THAT MAKE *WUDHU* NECESSARY

The conditions that make *wudhu wajib* are:
1. Being sane,
2. To have reached the age of puberty,
3. To be Muslim,
4. Having access to the use of enough water with which to perform *wudhu*,
5. The presence of *hadath*[52],
6. The absence of *haidh, nifaas*[53] and the shortage of time[54].

---

[49] It is narrated by Ameer Al-Mu'mineen Sayyiduna 'Uthman bin 'Affan 'Dhun-Noorain' ﷺ that Rasoolullah ﷺ said, "He who performs wudhu in the sunnah way, his sins leave his body even from under his nails." [Muslim]
It has also been mentioned, that Imam Abu Hanifah ﷺ initially ruled that used water (ma' musta'mal) is najas (impure) because he was able to see people's sins being washed away in that used water.

[50] It is narrated by Sayyiduna Abu Hurrairah ﷺ that Rasoolullah ﷺ said that on the Day of Judgement when my followers will be summoned the parts they wash during wudhu will be shining brightly, so those of you who can increase this brightness should do so. [Bukhari and Muslim] So Sayyiduna Abu Hurairah ﷺ would wash his arms all the way up to the shoulders in order to increase the glow on the Day of Judgement.

[51] Rasoolullah ﷺ said that cleanliness is half of faith, so it is essential for every Muslim to remain clean.

[52] Al-hadath al-asghar must be present, i.e. that he is not in wudhu already, because if he is already in wudhu then it won't be wajib for him to do wudhu again.

21

FARA'IDH

There are four *arkaan*[55] of *wudhu* and they are also its *fara'idh*[56]:
1. Washing the **face**[57],
2. Washing both **hands**, up to and including the elbows,
3. Performing *mas'h*[58] of a quarter of the **head**,
4. Washing both **feet** including the ankles.

CONDITIONS FOR PROPERLY DONE *WUDHU*

There are three conditions for the assurance of having performed *wudhu* properly:
1. That *taahir, mutahhir* water reaches all those parts of the body which are *fardh* to wash during *wudhu*,
2. That those things which are against *wudhu* such as *haidh* and *nifaas* etc. have stopped,
3. The absence of anything on the body that stops water from reaching the body such as fat and wax.

Memorise... ...the part of ayah number six of Surah Al-Maidah in which Allah ﷻ revealed the four fara'idh of wudhu.

يَا اَيُّهَا الَّذِيْنَ اٰمَنُوْا اِذَا قُمْتُمْ اِلَي الصَّلٰوةِ فَاغْسِلُوْا وُجُوْهَكُمْ وَ اَيْدِيَكُمْ اِلَي الْمَرَافِقِ وَ امْسَحُوْا بِرُؤُوْسِكُمْ وَ اَرْجُلَكُمْ اِلَي الْكَعْبَيْنِ...

Oh believing men and women, when you intend to stand for salah then wash your faces and your arms including the elbows, do mas'h of your heads, and wash your feet including the ankles.

---

[53] This means it is not wajib for a woman who is in haidh or nifaas to perform wudhu, although it is desirable for her in order to keep up the routine if she is in the habit of staying in wudhu.

[54] Shortage of time: This means those times when there is not enough time to do wudhu and you are allowed to do tayammum instead. For example: if a funeral prayer is about to begin and there isn't enough time to perform wudhu then you are allowed to do tayammum if you are not a close relative of the deceased. For more detail see the chapter on tayammum.

[55] (أركان) Arkaan: Plural of rukn meaning pillars. NOTE: The difference between a condition and a pillar: a condition exists before the action and the action cannot begin until the conditions are met. The pillars exist within the action and the action is incomplete and void without all the pillars.

[56] (فرائض) Fara'idh: Plural of fardh meaning obligations.

[57] The definition of the face is; in length, the area from the top of the forehead to below the chin; and in width, the area between the two earlobes.

[58] (مسح) Mas'h: Literally means to touch. In terms of fiqh it means wetting the hands and running over the head (or leather socks) during wudhu.

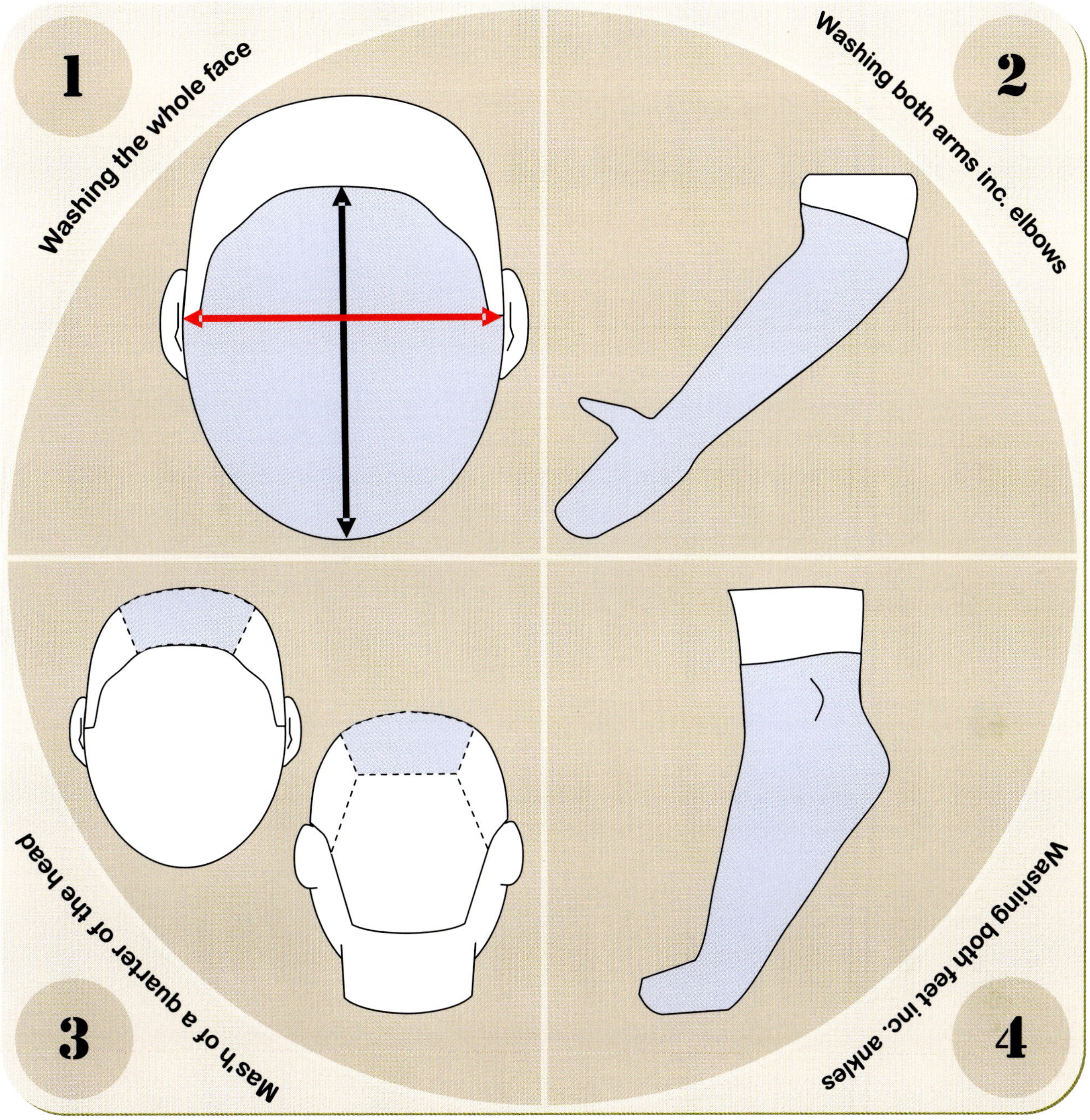

1 Washing the whole face

2 Washing both arms inc. elbows

3 Mas'h of a quarter of the head

4 Washing both feet inc. ankles

The diagram above shows the four fara'idh of wudhu in their correct order:
1. Washing all the face from hairline to chin and earlobe to earlobe.
2. Washing both arms up to and including the elbows.
3. Doing mas'h of ¼ of the head (the head is divided into four parts in the diagram to show one quarter, you must do mas'h of at least one of the four parts).
4. Washing both feet up to and including the ankles.

23

Lesson 10
Wudhu

THE *WAJIBAAT* OF *WUDHU*

- It is *wajib* to wash the exterior of a thick beard.

- It is *wajib* for the water to reach the skin in the case of a thin beard.

- It is not *wajib* for water to reach the hair of the beard which is outside the area of the face, nor that area which is concealed when the lips meet.

- If the fingers are joined together or the nails are overgrown so that they cover any part of the fingertips, or if there is anything beneath the nails that is a barrier for water such as flour dough, then it is *wajib* to wash beneath it. Dirt (such as dead skin) is not a barrier for water.

- It is *wajib* to move a tight fitting ring from its place, during *wudhu*.

- If it is painful to wash the wounds of the feet (such as cracked skin around the heal area), it is permissible to just pass water over any medication applied to the wounds.

- It is not necessary to re-do *mas'h* of the head, nor to wash it after having it shaved. Neither is it necessary to wash the respective areas again after cutting the nails or trimming the moustache.

KEY WORD

Wajib pl. wajibaat (واجب ج واجبات)

The word wajib has two meanings, a literal one and a technical one in fiqh.

Literal meaning: an obligatory/necessary act.
Technical meaning: In fiqh, the word wajib describes the grading of those actions which are between fardh and sunnah. These are actions which are not directly and explicitly commanded, like fardh actions - but their command is implied.

There are no wajibaat in wudhu as such, the word wajib in this case is used in its literal sense because the actions described in this lesson are necessary in order to be certain that the fara'idh have been completed fully and correctly.

Lesson 11
Wudhu

THE *SUNAN*[59] OF *WUDHU*

There are eighteen *sunan* of *wudhu*:

1. To wash both hands including the wrists,

2. To begin with the name of Allah 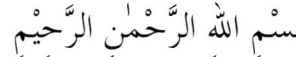 by saying:

    بِسْمِ اللهِ الرَّحْمٰنِ الرَّحِيْمِ
    Bismillahir-rahmanir-rahim[60]

3. To brush the teeth with a *miswaak*[61] at the beginning of *wudhu* (or even using the index finger, if a *miswaak* or toothbrush is not available),

4. To rinse the mouth with water three times, even if one handful of water is used,

5. To rinse the nose three times, with three handfuls of water,

6. For someone who is not fasting, to be thorough in rinsing the mouth and nose[62],

7. To do *khilaal*[63] of a thick beard with one handful of water from beneath,

8. To do *khilaal* of the fingers,

9. To wash each part three times,

10. To cover the whole head when doing *mas'h*, once,

11. To do *mas'h* of the ears even if it is with the same water as the water for the *mas'h* of the head,

12. To scrub the areas washed,

---

[59] (سنن) Sunan: Plural of Sunnah.

[60] I begin with the name of Allah, the Most Kind, the Ever Merciful.

[61] (مسواك) Miswaak: A kind of toothbrush made from the branches or roots of certain plants containing natural cleaning elements. There are many benefits associated with Miswaak and many ahadith stress upon its importance.

[62] For someone who is not fasting, because for someone who is fasting there is danger of the water passing beyond the throat and breaking the fast.

[63] (خلال) Khilaal: To comb or run the fingers through something.

13. To be continuous[64],

14. To make *niyyah*[65],

15. To wash in the same order that Allah ﷻ has revealed in The Holy Qur'an,

16. To begin washing each part from the right hand side and from the tips of the fingers in the case of the hands,

17. To begin *mas'h* from the front of the head,

18. To do *mas'h* of the back of the neck, not the throat.

THINK!

All the eighteen sunan mentioned above are proven through authentic narrations mentioned in various sahih books of hadith. It paints a picture of how Rasoolullah ﷺ performed wudhu. When we do wudhu we should remember all these sunan and see if we are collecting the thawab of acting on the blessed way of Rasoolullah ﷺ.

Each sunnah should teach us deeper love of The Beloved Messenger of Allah ﷺ. Love, honour and respect for The Prophet ﷺ is the essence of our deen and imaan, just think of the scene when the blessed companions ﷺ would compete with one another to catch the water used by Rasoolullah ﷺ for wudhu before it touched the ground, then they would rub this on their faces and bodies for barakah. SubhanAllah!

Sunnah pl. sunan (سنة ج سنن)

The word sunnah has many meanings. Apart from the literal meaning, the scholars of hadith, usul and fiqh have all given technical definitions according to their specialist subjects.

Literal meaning: a path or way.
Technical meaning: In the science of hadith, the word sunnah means a saying, an action, the silent approval or the description of Rasoolullah ﷺ. It also includes the way of the rightly guided Caliphs ﷺ because Rasoolullah ﷺ said hold onto my way and the way of my Caliphs. In the field of fiqh it is the grading of those actions which are below wajib and above mustahab.

---

[64] This means to do wudhu from beginning to end without a break so all the parts are wet at the end of the wudhu.

[65] (نيّة) Niyyah: To make the intention of making those things permissible, that are not permissible without wudhu (such as salah and touching The Holy Qur'an).

Lesson 12
Wudhu

THE *AADAAB* OF WUDHU

Fourteen things are *mustahab* in *wudhu*:
1. To sit on a raised place,
2. To face the *Qiblah*.
3. Not to seek help from another person without a good reason,
4. Not to speak of worldly affairs,
5. To say the *niyyah* with the tongue as well as having it in the heart,
6. To say a *masnoon*[66] *du'a*,
7. To say بسم الله الرحمن الرحيم when washing each part,
8. To insert the little fingers in the ears when performing *mas'h* of the ears,
9. To move around a loose-fitting ring if you are wearing one,
10. To rinse the mouth and nose using the right hand,
11. To clean the nose with the left hand,
12. To perform *wudhu* before the start of the time for *salah*,
13. To say the *shahaadatain*[67] after *wudhu*,
14. To drink any left over water whilst standing after *wudhu* and saying the following prayer:

اَللّٰهُمَّ اجْعَلْنِيْ مِنْ التَّوَّابِيْنَ وَ اجْعَلْنِيْ مِنْ الْمُتَطَهِّرِيْنَ

Allahumma-ja'alnee min-at-tawwabeena wa-ja'alni min-al-mutatahhireen.

O Allah! Make me among those who beg for forgiveness, and make me among those who are well purified.

---

[66] (الدعاء المسنون) Masnoon Dua: A supplication said by the Messenger of Allah ﷺ.

[67] (شهادتين) To say the shahaadatain means to say these words:

اَشْهَدُ اَنْ لَّا اِلٰهَ اِلَّااللهُ وَ اَشْهَدُ اَنَّ مُحَمَّداً عَبْدُهُ وَ رَسُوْلُهُ ○

"Ash-hadu anlaa ilaha illallhu wa ash-hadu anna Muhammadan 'abduhu wa rasooluh."

I testify that there is no deity except Allah ﷻ and Muhammad ﷺ is His chosen servant and His final messenger.

It is narrated by Ameer Al-Mu'mineen Sayyiduna 'Umar bin Al-Khattaab ﷺ that Rasoolullah ﷺ said whoever performs wudhu properly and recites the shahaadatain, then all eight gates of Paradise are opened for him and he may enter through whichever one he chooses. [Muslim]

THE *MAKROOHAAT* OF *WUDHU*

Six things are *makrooh* whilst performing *wudhu*:
1. To use more water than is needed,
2. To use less water than is needed,
3. To hit the water on the face with force,
4. To speak of worldly affairs whilst performing *wudhu*,
5. To seek help from another person in performing *wudhu* without a good reason,
6. To perform *mas'h* of the head three times, using fresh water each time.

Exercise: Memorise the Arabic text of the du'a recited after wudhu, together with its meaning.

Adab pl. Aadaab (ادب ج آداب)

Literal meaning: good manners, etiquettes, qualities.
Technical meaning: In fiqh it means mustahab actions, those actions which are below sunnah and above mubah. These are those actions which Rasoolullah ﷺ sometimes did do and other times didn't do. Other words for this type of action include mustahab and mandoob.

These are preferred actions so if you do them you will receive thawab, but if you leave them you will not be punished.

Makrooh pl. Makroohaat (مكروه ج مكروهات)

Literal meaning: disliked, disapproved, unpleasant.
Technical meaning: According to the scholars of fiqh, a makrooh action can be defined in several ways.
a. Its disapproval is found in the texts but its permissibilty is also found.
b. It is permissible in essence but it is close to something which is not allowed.
c. Leaving it is better than doing it. The one who leaves it will be rewarded but the one who does it will not be punished.

There are two types of makrooh action:
1. *Makrooh tahrimi*. It is closer to haram than halal and it is disapproved. The one who does it will be told off but will not be punished. When the word makrooh is used on its own, it usually means this type.
2. *Makrooh tanzihi*. It is closer to halal than haram but it is disliked. The one who does it will not be shown disapproval.

28

Lesson 13
Wudhu

THE TYPES OF *WUDHU*

Wudhu is of three types:

1. The first type is **Fardh** upon a *muh'dith*[68] for:
   a. Performing *salah* (even if it is *nafl salah*[69] or *salah-tul-janazah*[70] or *sajdah-tut-tilawah*[71]),
   b. Touching The Holy Qur'an (even if it is one *ayah*).

2. The second type is **wajib**, for performing *tawaf*[72] of The Holy Ka'bah[73].

GROUP EXERCISE

Before going on to look at the examples of when it is mustahab to do wudhu, in groups of 3-4, make a spider diagram showing those times when you think it is good to do wudhu and then compare your list with the one on the next page.

---

[68] (محدث) A muh'dith is a person in the state of minor impurity

[69] (نفل صلوٰة) Nafl, or voluntary, salah means extra prayers offered besides fardh and wajib prayers.

[70] (صلوٰة الجنازه) Salah-tul-janazah means the funeral prayer

[71] (سجدة التلاوة) Sajdah-tut-tilawah is the prostration of recitation. There are 14 verses in the Holy Quran, if they are recited or heard then sajdah becomes wajib (details in Kitaab As-Salah *Insha Allah*).

[72] (طواف) Tawaf means making seven anti-clockwise circles around The Holy Ka'bah.

[73] (كعبة) Ka'bah. This is the black cube shaped building in Al-Masjid Al-Haram in Makkah Al-Mukarramah.

29

3. The third type is **mustahab**:
   a. For sleeping in a state of purity and after waking from sleep,
   b. For remaining constantly in a state of purity,
   c. For gaining greater *thawab* by performing *wudhu* whilst already in a state of *wudhu*,
   d. After backbiting, lying or tale telling,
   e. After committing any sin,
   f. After reciting bad (vulgar) poetry,
   g. After laughing out loud (outside of *salah*[74]),
   h. After bathing a dead body, and after carrying it,
   i. At the time of every *salah*,
   j. Before bathing when in a state of *janabah*,
   k. For a *junubi*[75] before eating, drinking, sleeping or intercourse,
   l. When in anger[76],
   m. When reading[77] The Holy *Qur'an* or *hadith*[78], or when narrating it,
   n. When learning knowledge[79],
   o. When saying the *adhan*[80] or *iqamah*[81],
   p. When visiting the tomb of The Holy Prophet ﷺ,
   q. When staying in '*Arafah*[82],
   r. When performing *sa'ee*[83] between *safa*[84] and *marwah*[85],
   s. After eating camel meat,
   t. To escape a disagreement between the scholars, such as after touching a woman[86].

---

[74] If someone laughs out loud within salah then this breaks the wudhu so he would have to perform wudhu again. Here, however, the situation is regarding laughing out loud- outside of salah.

[75] (الجنبى) A junubi is a person who is in the state of janabah (major impurity).

[76] Rasoolullah ﷺ said that anger is from the Shaytan and the Shaytan is made of fire; fire is extinguished by water; so you should perform wudhu when you are angry. [Abu Dawood]

[77] Note, it says reading not touching, because you must do wudhu to touch The Holy Qur'an, here it means reciting from memory or reading without touching The Holy Qur'an.

[78] (الحديث) Hadith. Sayings of the Holy Prophet ﷺ and his companions ﷺ.

[79] This means Islamic knowledge or any other knowledge which is used to understand or help the religion or which will bring benefit to people.

[80] (أذان) Adhan is the call to prayer

[81] (إقامة) Iqamah is a minor version of the Adhan recited before the congregational prayer to indicate the beginning of the salah.

[82] (عرفة) 'Arafah is the area in which the pilgrim must remain for a while for the completion of Hajj.

[83] (السعى) Sa'ee means walking between the two mountains, Safa and Marwa in Makkah Al-Mukarramah.

[84] (الصفا) Safa is the name of a mountain in Makkah Al-Mukarramah from which sa'ee begins.

[85] (المروة) Marwah is the name of a mountain in Makkah Al-Mukarramah, at which sa'ee ends.

[86] It is the view of Imam Shaf'i ﷺ that if a man touches a woman then his wudhu breaks. This is not the view of Imam Abu Hanifah ﷺ. So it is best to perform wudhu to get out of this disagreement between the scholars.

Lesson 14
Wudhu

THE THINGS THAT BREAK *WUDHU*

Wudhu is broken by twelve things:
1. Anything which comes out of the two passages[87], except wind from the front[88],
2. The childbirth where no blood is seen,
3. Any flowing *najasah*, which exits the body, such as blood or pus,
4. Vomiting, of food, water, clotted blood or yellow water, when it is one mouthful[89] or more. When there are many incidents of vomiting because of one cause, then the total amount will be taken into account,
5. When there is more blood in the saliva, or if the blood and saliva are of equal amounts,
6. Falling asleep when the backside is not resting firmly on the ground[90],
7. When the backside of the sleeping person rises from the ground before he wakes up (even if he doesn't actually fall over),
8. Unconsciousness,
9. Insanity,
10. Intoxication,
11. The laughing out loud (*Qahqahah*) of an adult during a *salah* that contains *rukoo'* and *sujood* whilst being awake[91],
12. For a man to touch the private parts of a woman with his erect penis without anything separating the two.

Did You Know?

In the Arabic language there are three words to describe laughter.
1. **Qahqahah.** This means to laugh out loud so that the people around you can hear your laughter.
2. **Dihk.** This is when the people around you cannot hear your laughter, you can hear it yourself.
3. **Tabassum.** This means smiling, so there is no noise and your teeth do not show either.

---

[87] (سبيلين) This means the two passages which are part of the excretory system, through which urine and faeces leaves the body.
[88] This refers to women only; wind from the front does not break the wudhu.
[89] When the vomit cannot be stopped easily and is forced out of the mouth, it is more than a mouthful.
[90] This means sleeping whilst lying on the side, for example. If a person fell asleep whilst standing up, his wudhu would not be broken, even though his backside is not resting on the ground.
[91] If it is a child, or Salah-tul-Janazah, or he is asleep then his wudhu is not broken.

Lesson 15
Wudhu

THE THINGS THAT DON'T BREAK *WUDHU*

Wudhu is not broken by ten things:
1. The appearance of blood or pus when it does not spread from its origin,
2. The falling of meat from any part of the body without bleeding occurring, for example *al-irq al-madani*[92], which is called *rishtah*[93] in Persian,
3. If an insect comes out of a wound, the ear or the nose,
4. Touching the private parts,
5. Touching a woman,
6. Vomiting less than one mouthful,
7. Vomiting mucus, even in large amounts,
8. When a sleeping person bows over so much that there is a possibility of his backside coming off the ground[94],
9. Sleeping whilst leaning against an object (even if he would fall over if this object was removed) as long as the backside is firmly resting on the ground[95],
10. Falling asleep during *rukooh* or *sujood*[96] whilst in *salah*, when this *rukooh* or *sujood* is according to the *sunnah*.

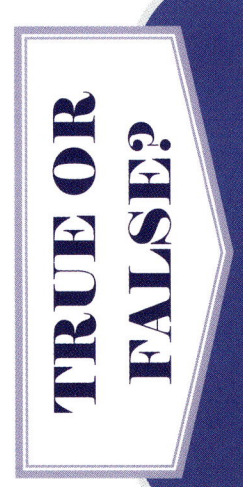

TRUE OR FALSE?

1. Every childbirth breaks the mother's wudhu.
2. Vomiting half a mouthful of mucus three times on one occasion breaks the wudhu.
3. A small paper-cut on the finger will break the wudhu.
4. Touching a woman breaks the wudhu.
5. If you faint, your wudhu is broken.
6. If you do tabassum in salah it breaks your wudhu.

---

[92] (العرق المدني) Al-irq al-madani is the name given to a condition in which a pimple appears in the surface of the skin and when it bursts then a small amount of meat comes out a little at a time without any flow of blood.

[93] (رشته) Rishtah is the Persian name for al-irq al-madani. In Urdu it is called "naaro".

[94] Due to uncertainty the wudhu will not break.

[95] The point to note here is that, the backside is resting on the ground, which is why the wudhu will not break.

[96] (السجده/السجود) Sajdah and sujood are both used to mean prostration, like in salah.

Lesson 16
Ghusl

THE THINGS THAT MAKE *GHUSL*[97] *FARDH*

Ghusl becomes *fardh* with any one of seven things:
1. The appearance of *mani*[98] on the outside of the body when it leaves its origin with force (even without intercourse[99]),
2. If the *hashfa*[100] disappears inside any of the two passages of another person[101],
3. Releasing *mani* in the case of having intercourse with an animal or a dead body[102],
4. The presence of a watery liquid after awaking from sleep[103], if the penis was not erect at the time of falling asleep[104],
5. The presence of wetness which he thinks could be *mani* after recovering from intoxication or unconsciousness,
6. The end of *haidh*[105],
7. The end of *nifaas*[106],

...even if any of the above have occurred before accepting Islam[107].

It is *fardh kifaayah*[108] to bathe a dead person.

---

[97] (الغُسل) Ghusl literally means to bathe, in fiqh it means bathing in such a way that the fara'idh of ghusl are completed.

[98] (المنيّ) Mani means semen

[99] Like having a wet-dream.

[100] (الحشفة) Hashfa is the name given to the tip of the penis.

[101] It should be noted here that the ONLY passage where any man's hashfa should disappear into is the front passage of his wife. The author has left his statement open to include such low and evil acts as sodomy because unfortunately there are some individuals who, despite being Muslims, will engage in such filthy, haram acts. May Allah ﷻ protect all Muslims from these immoral and extremely sinful acts, ameen.

[102] Again, it should be noted that both of these acts are forbidden and haram for Muslims. If some person commited these vile acts he would earn the anger of Allah ﷻ and make himself worthy of being punished in the hell-fire. Such a person should seek Allah's ﷻ mercy and forgiveness and refrain from these acts.

[103] Because sleep is a time of relaxation and increased sexual appetite, it is most likely that this liquid is mani.

[104] If the penis was erect at the time of going to sleep then it is more likely that the liquid is mazi and ghusl would not be fardh, rather just wudhu.

[105] (الحيض) Haidh is the monthly menstruation or periods.

[106] (النِّفاس) Nifaas is the period of bleeding after childbirth (Post-natal bleeding).

[107] What is meant here is that if any of the above 7 things applied to a non-Muslim and then this person accepted Islam it would still be fardh for that person to perform ghusl, even though the shariah did not apply to him/her at the time that one of these things occurred.

[108] (الفرض الكفاية) Fardh kifaayah means a collective duty. That action which is obligatory on all the members of a community; if no one does it then they are all sinful and answerable to Allah, however if some members of that community carry it out then the burden is removed from the whole community.

Lesson 17
Ghusl

THE THINGS THAT DON'T MAKE *GHUSL FARDH*

1. *Mazee*[109],
2. *Wadee*[110],
3. Having a wet dream without ejaculation,
4. Childbirth without bleeding,
5. Entering the penis into a woman's private part whilst the penis is covered by something (such as cloth) that stops the feeling of pleasure[111],
6. Having *huqnah*[112] (enema) done,
7. Entering a finger or similar object into either of the two paths[113],
8. Intercourse with an animal[114] without ejaculation,
9. Intercourse with a deceased person[115] without ejaculation,
10. Intercourse with a virgin whose hymen remains intact without ejaculation[116].

	Mani	*Mazee*	*Wadee*
When is it released?	At the point of climax during intercourse	Prior to intercourse whilst in a state of excitement	After or before urinating.
Is it released with force?	✓	✗	✗
Does it make *ghusl fardh*?	✓	✗	✗
Does it have a smell?	✓	✗	✗
Is it necessary to have an erection for it to be released?	✓	✗	✗
Does the erection finish after it is released?	✓	✗	✗

---

[109] Mazee. This is a whitish, watery liquid, without any smell, that is released without force prior to intercourse, while in a state of excitement (during foreplay).

[110] Wadee. This is a watery liquid that has a similar appearance to semen and has no smell. It may be released without force in the form of a few drops after or before urinating.

[111] If the cloth etc. were not there then ghusl would be fardh.

[112] Huqnah means injection or enema in English. It means inserting a liquid (water solution or medication) into the anal passage in order to induce bowel movement as well as treating other diseases.

[113] The two paths are vagina and anus. This may be the case if a medical instrument is inserted into either of these passages such as having a smear test done to check for cervical cancer.

[114] It should be noted that intercourse with animals is a haram act in Islam, and anyone who does this will be committing a grave sin. If, however, someone does do this haram and filthy act then ghusl does not become wajib unless he releases semen and he should repent and seek forgiveness for this sin.

[115] As above, this is also a forbidden act and a major sin, however, the same rule applies, that ghusl becomes fardh only when he releases semen and likewise he should seek forgiveness for this.

[116] This means that if a man has intercourse with his wife who is a virgin and her hymen remains intact then ghusl will not become fardh on them both until they release mani. This is because the hymen prevents the male and female private parts from fully meeting.

TO BATHE OR NOT TO BATHE ?

Read the statements below and decide if ghusl will become fardh in each of the situations

'Amr wakes up and finds a smelly, sticky liquid on his clothes. Is ghusl fardh for him?

Rabia has just started her monthly cycle, her friend Nasreen told her that ghusl becomes fardh on her as soon as her period begins, is this true?

Tariq went to see the doctor due to a pain in his lower abdomen. The doctor inserted a camera up his back passage. Will Tariq have to do ghusl when he returns home?

shafiq's auntie has had a baby and she says no blood was seen during the delivery. Her grandma says she must rest for forty days and cannot pray until doing ghusl on the 40th day. Is this true?

Lesson 18
Ghusl

THE *FARA'IDH* OF *GHUSL*

There are three *fara'idh* of *ghusl*:

1. To rinse the mouth[117] with water,
2. To rinse the nose[118] with water,
3. To wash the entire body once.

Care needs to be taken in completing the following to ensure that the *fardh* of washing the <u>entire</u> body is completed properly:

1. To wash the inside of the *kulfah*[119] if it is possible without discomfort/difficulty,
2. To wash the naval[120],
3. To wash the inside of any hole in the body that hasn't sealed up[121],
4. For a man to wash the inside of his plaits by opening the hair[122]. A woman does not have to open and wash the inside of her plaits as long as the water reaches the roots of the hair[123],
5. To wash the skin beneath the beard, moustache and eyebrows[124],
6. For a woman to wash her *farj al-khaarij*[125].

---

[117] The water must reach the throat (حلق) when rinsing the mouth but should not pass beyond it. If someone is fasting then it is advised not to be too thorough in this rinsing due to the fear of breaking the fast if the water passes beyond the throat.

[118] The water must reach the hard part of the bone in the nose (beyond the cartilage).

[119] (الكلفة) Kulfah is the name of the foreskin on a man's private parts which is usually removed during circumcision. If someone has not been circumcised and finds it painful to move the foreskin to pass water beneath it then it is permissible to leave it because the shariah does not seek to create difficulties for people.

[120] Because the navel is on the exterior of the body, therefore its washing is fardh. It cannot be washed properly until it is opened and water is passed into it as thoroughly as possible.

[121] Such as a hole from a piercing or injury etc.

[122] A man must open his plaits because it is not part of a man's zeenah (beauty) to have plaits, also a man should not have hair longer than shoulder-length.

[123] Women have been given this permission because it is part of a woman's zeenah to have long hair and a woman is forbidden from having hair shorter than shoulder length (because of resemblance with men). Thus most women have long hair so this is to create ease for them.

[124] In the Qur'an, when seeking purity from janabah is mentioned, it says, فَاطَّهَّرُوا which means be <u>thoroughly</u> cleansed, so the scholars say that when performing fardh ghusl even if one hair remains dry then the fardh is not completed. This is why it is important to make sure that the skin behind the moustache, beard and eyebrows is washed properly.

[125] (الفرج الخارج) Al-farj al-khaarij is the outer part of a woman's private parts. A woman has two parts to her private part, the outer and inner part. Just like it is fardh to wash the inside of the mouth but not to pass the water beyond the throat, likewise it is necessary for a woman to wash her farj al-khaarij (outer private part) but not her farj ad-daakhil (inner private part).

GROUP EXERCISE

Working in groups of 3-4, complete the table below, showing a comparison between wudhu and ghusl. Each person in the group must fill their own table but you may discuss with your group members. Ask your teacher if you are unsure.

	Wudhu	Ghusl
How many fara'idh does it have?		
Is rinsing the mouth and nose one of the fara'idh?		
Which source of fiqh do we know these fara'idh from?		
Which type of hadath (impurity) does it remove?		
Can you enter the masjid if it is fardh upon you?		
Can you touch the Qur'an if it is fardh upon you?		
Can you pray salah if it is fardh upon you?		

Lesson 19
Ghusl

THE *SUNAN* OF *GHUSL*

There are twelve *sunan* in *ghusl*:
1. To begin with *tasmiyyah*[126],
2. To make *niyyah*[127] of purity,
3. To wash both hands including the wrists[128],
4. If there is any *najasah* on the body, then to wash it off separately[129],
5. To wash the private parts (*istinjaa*),
6. To do *wudhu* like *wudhu* is done for *salah*, washing each part three times and performing *mas'h* of the head; but washing the feet should be left until the end if he is standing in a place where the water collects around the feet due to poor drainage[130],
7. To run water over the whole body three times. If he submerges himself in running water (or which comes under the same ruling as running water[131]) and remains in it for a short while, he has completed this *sunnah*[132],
8. To begin with the head when pouring the water,
9. To wash the right shoulder,
10. To wash the left shoulder,
11. To scrub the body,
12. To complete all this *ghusl* by washing continuously[133].

HOW RASOOLULLAH ﷺ DID GHUSL:

It is narrated by Umm Al-Mu'mineen Sayyidah 'Aisha ﷺ that when Rasoolullah ﷺ would bathe from janabah he would begin by washing both hands and do istinjaa', then he would do wudhu like the wudhu for salah. He would then wet his fingers and run them through the roots of his hair, before pouring water on his head three times. Finally he would run water over his whole body. [Bukhari and Muslim]

---

[126] (التسميّة) Tasmiyyah means saying the name of Allah ﷻ by reciting: بسم الله الرحمن الرحيم

[127] (النيّة) Niyyah means intention.

[128] The hands should be washed first up to the wrists because if they are not clean how will they scrub the rest of the body and clean it?

[129] This means to wash the najasah off first, before beginning ghusl.

[130] If the person is in a place where the used water collects around the feet then he should leave the washing of the feet until the very end and wash the feet when he steps out of this area.

[131] That water which is more than 10 × 10 yards and has no najasah in it is treated like running water, even if it is still.

[132] The purpose of washing the body three times is to be sure that all the areas have been washed. If he submerges himself in running water then this will be enough to ensure that the water has reached all the areas that need to be washed so he has achieved the purpose of the sunnah.

[133] This means not letting one part dry before washing the next.

Lesson 20
Ghusl

THE *AADAAB* OF *GHUSL*

The *mustahabbaat* of *ghusl* are like those of *wudhu* except to not face the *Qiblah* because most people are fully undressed when bathing[134]. The *makroohaat* of *ghusl* are the same as those of *wudhu*.

THOSE OCCASIONS WHEN *GHUSL* IS *SUNNAH*

It is *sunnah* to perform *ghusl* on four occasions:
1. *Salah-tul-Jumu'ah*[135],
2. *Salah-tul-Eidain*[136],
3. Wearing the *ihram*[137],
4. For *hujjaaj*[138], in *'Arafah*[139], after *zawaal*[140].

THE TIMES WHEN IT IS *MUSTAHAB* TO PERFORM *GHUSL*

It is *mustahab* to perform *ghusl* for sixteen things.
1. For that person who became a Muslim whilst in a state of purity[141],
2. For that person who reaches *balooghah*[142] by age,
3. For that person who recoveres from insanity,
4. After having *hijamah*[143] (cupping) done,
5. After bathing a deceased person,

---

[134] It is disrespectful to face the Qiblahh or to turn the back to the Qiblahh whilst being undressed.

[135] (صلوٰة الجمعة) Salah-tul-Jumu'ah is the name of the Friday congregational prayer.

[136] (صلوٰة العيدين) Salah-tul-Eidain is the prayer of the two Eids, Eid Al-Fitr and Eid Al-Adha.

[137] (الاحرام) Ihram means the two white sheets worn during hajj/umrah.

[138] (حجاج) Hujjaaj is the plural of haaji, meaning one who performs hajj, i.e. the pilgrim.

[139] (عرفة) 'Arafah is the name of a plain near the city of Makkah. The Hujjaaj must come and stay here on the 9th of Dhul-Hijjah in order to complete the hajj, staying in 'Arafah is one of the fara'idh of Hajj. It is this place where the tawbah of Prophet Adam ﷺ was accepted and it is also the place where people will be gathered on the Day of Judgement.

[140] (زوال) Zawaal: after the sun reaches the highest point in the sky and then begins its downward journey towards sunset, i.e. the point after true midday (not according to clocks but according to the sun cycle). This is also the beginning time of Zuhr salah.

[141] If someone accepts Islam in a state of impurity then it would be fardh for him/her to perform ghusl, not mustahab.

[142] (بلوغة) Balooghah. Adulthood/puberty. Adulthood can be reached in two ways:
- The first is when a boy or girl has a wet dream for the first time or if a girl has her first period or becomes pregnant. In any of these cases ghusl is fardh.
- The second way is balooghah by age. This is if a boy or girl reaches the age of fifteen without any of the above occurring, in this case it is mustahab to do ghusl.

[143] (حجامة) Hijamah means having dirty blood removed for medical reasons by having small incisions made on certain parts of the body, in English it is called cupping or phlebotomy or bloodletting.

6. On *Laylah-tul-Bara'ah*[144],
7. On *Laylah-tul-Qadr*[145],
8. When entering *Madinah-tur-Rasool* ﷺ[146],
9. When staying in *Muzdalifah*[147] on the morning of *Yawm An-Nahr*[148],
10. When entering the holy city of *Makkah*[149],
11. For *Tawaaf Az-Ziyarah*[150],
12. For *Salah-tul-Kusoof*[151],
13. For *Salah-tul-Istisqaa*[152],
14. At the time of fear,
15. At the time of extreme darkness during the day,
16. During a storm[153].

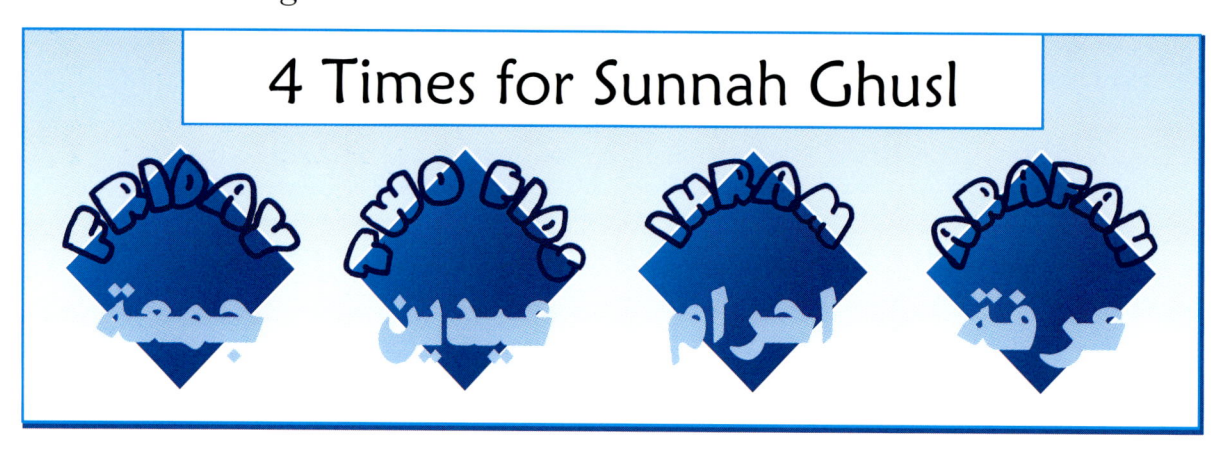

4 Times for Sunnah Ghusl

FRIDAY — جمعة
TWO EIDS — عيدين
IHRAM — احرام
ARAFAH — عرفة

---

[144] (ليلة البراءة) Laylah-tul-Bara'ah: according to most scholars this is on the 15th of Sha'baan. Bara'ah means freedom. It is called the Night of Freedom because on this night Allah sets those Muslims free from the Hell fire who beg for his pardon and forgiveness.

[145] (ليلة القدر) Laylah-tul-Qadr means the Night of Power, most likely one of the odd nights amongst the last ten nights of Ramadhan. Worship in this night is better than the worship of a thousand months as stated in the Hoy Quran in Surah Al-Qadr, ayah 2.

[146] It is mustahab to do ghusl for entering the city of The Holy Prophet Muhammad ﷺ in order to show respect and honour to Rasoolullah ﷺ and his city.

[147] (مزدلفة) Muzdalifah is the name of a place where pilgrims usually spend the night after stopping at 'Arafah during the Hajj. It is mustahab to perform ghusl here after Fajar time begins.

[148] (يوم النحر) Yawm An-Nahr is the 10th day of the Islamic month of Dhul-Hijjah when the Hujjaaj sacrifice an animal in the way of Allah ﷻ.

[149] (مكه) Makkah, also spelt Mecca; this is to show honour and respect to this city because Allah ﷻ has sworn by this city in the Holy Qur'an and it is one of the holiest cities on earth.

[150] (طواف الزيارة) Tawaaf Az-Ziyarah is one of the pillars of Hajj and must be done to complete the Hajj. This tawaaf is performed by pilgrims any time after sunrise on the 10th of Dhul Hijjah. It is mustahab to attain thorough cleanliness by doing ghusl to honour the sanctity of the Holy Ka'bah and the fact that this tawaaf is fardh.

[151] (صلوٰة الكسوف) Salah-tul-Kusoof is a special salah that is performed during a solar eclipse.

[152] (صلوٰة الاستسقاء) Salah-tul-Istisqaa is the name of a salah that is especially performed to ask Allah ﷻ for rain at the time of drought.

[153] During occasions of fear, darkness or severe storms etc, as mentioned in hadith, the Muslims would pray to Allah ﷻ and beg for forgiveness of their sins because these times are reminders of the Last Day and also of the punishments that destroyed many nations before us. It is preferred that a Muslim should purify himself thoroughly before praying at a time like this, so it is mustahab to do ghusl.

Lesson 21
Tayammum

TAYAMMUM – WHAT IS IT?

The literal meaning of *tayammum* is "to intend."
The technical definition in *fiqh* is: **the mas'h of the face and the hands using mutahhir (purifying) earth with the intention of purity.**

Tayammum is a blessing from *Allah* ﷻ; it is a way of creating ease for anyone who is unable to use water to perform *wudhu* or *ghusl*. It is sometimes called dry ablution in English.

Allah ﷻ has revealed the ruling regarding *tayammum* in the same *ayah* which describes the four *fara'idh* of *wudhu*; Surah Al-Maidah, ayah 6:

وَاِنْ كُنْتُمْ جُنُبًا فَاطَّهَّرُوْا ۚ وَاِنْ كُنْتُمْ مَّرْضٰۤى اَوْ عَلٰى سَفَرٍ اَوْ جَآءَ اَحَدٌ مِّنْكُمْ مِّنَ الْغَآئِطِ اَوْ لٰمَسْتُمُ النِّسَآءَ فَلَمْ تَجِدُوْا مَآءً فَتَيَمَّمُوْا صَعِيْدًا طَيِّبًا فَامْسَحُوْا بِوُجُوْهِكُمْ وَاَيْدِيْكُمْ مِّنْهُ ۚ

...And if you are in the state of major impurity, then purify yourselves thoroughly; And if you are ill or on a journey or one of you comes back from answering the call of nature or you have intercourse with your women, and you do not find water; then do tayammum with clean earth, wiping your faces and your arms with it...

Memorise... ...this part of ayah number 6 of Surah Al-Maidah and its meaning in which Allah ﷻ revealed the ruling of tayammum.

HOW THE RULING OF *TAYAMMUM* CAME ABOUT

Allah ﷻ also mentions *tayammum* in almost exactly the same words in *ayah* 43 of *Surah An-Nisaa*. The cause of revelation of this *ayah* is very interesting and full of many lessons for the believers.

During the fourth year of *hijrah*, the Battle of *Mustalaq* took place. On the way back from this battle the Muslims camped overnight in a valley where there was no water. The next morning as the Muslim army was about to leave, the beloved wife of *Rasoolullah* ﷺ *Umm Al-Mu'mineen*,[154] *Sayyidah A'isha Siddeeqah* ﷺ discovered that her necklace was missing. This held up the departure of the Muslims because the companions began to search for the necklace.

As the Muslims were in a place where no water was available, *Allah* ﷻ revealed *ayah* 43 of *Surah An-Nisaa*, giving the Muslims permission to do *tayammum*.

Asyad bin Hudhair ﷺ said to *Sayyidah A'isha Siddeeqah* ﷺ, O daughter of *Abu Bakr*, this is not your first *barakah* (blessing), meaning that the Muslims have received many blessing through you.

The necklace was eventually found under the camel of *Sayyidah A'isha Siddeeqah* ﷺ when it was made to stand.

GROUP EXERCISE

Before going further, working in groups of 3-4, discuss and write down at least 3 lessons we can learn from this incident.

_____
_____
_____
_____
_____
_____
_____

---

[154] This means *mother of the believers*. It is a title given to all the wives of Rasoolullah ﷺ.

THE LESSONS WE LEARN FROM THIS *AYAH*

There was much hidden wisdom behind why the necklace was lost and why the Keeper of *Allah's* secret treasures, His beloved and final Messenger did not reveal the whereabouts of the lost necklace.

- The fact that the whole army extended its stay in this valley due to the necklace of *Sayyidah A'isha* is an indication of her honour and rank.
- The companions search for the necklace shows us that it is an honour for a Muslim to serve the family of *Rasoolullah*.
- Then the revelation of the ruling of *tayammum* shows how great the rewards are that *Allah* showers upon the believers when they sincerely serve the family of The Holy Prophet because all the Muslims can take benefit from the ruling of *tayammum* until the Day of Judgement.
- The wives of The Messenger of *Allah* are called *"Ummahaat al-mu'mineen"* which means the mothers of the believers. So by serving *Sayyidah A'isha* the companions taught us an important lesson that we should always serve our parents, even if it means going out of our way and going to extra lengths to do so.
- The *ayah* also talks about "answering the call of nature" and "sleeping with your partners" when describing the *muhdith* and *junubi*. But *Allah* has mentioned this in a very subtle and elegant manner rather than using crude or vulgar language, teaching us not to be rude in our speech.
- Sometimes we become impatient and upset with circumstances in our lives because we can't see any immediate benefits of the situations that *Allah* creates for us, but we must always remember that there is wisdom in all the decisions *Allah* has ordained for us. It is our job to be patient and content with what we receive in this life.
- We, the *Ahl As-Sunnah* are blessed with the love of *Allah's* beloved Messenger and all those people, places and things related to him which includes his family and companions (May Allah be pleased with them all).

مَوْلَايَ صَلِّ وَ سَلِّمْ دَائِمًا اَبَدًا،
عَلٰى حَبِيْبِكَ خَيْرِ الْخَلْقِ كُلِّهِمْ

مَوْلَايَ صَلِّ وَ سَلِّمْ دَائِمًا اَبَدًا،
عَلَى النَّبِيِّ وَ اَهْلِ الْبَيْتِ كُلِّهِمْ

MY LORD, SEND BLESSINGS AND GREETINGS FOREVER AND ETERNALLY, NEVER ENDING. UPON YOUR BELOVED, THE BEST OF ALL CREATION.

MY LORD, SEND BLESSINGS AND GREETINGS FOREVER AND ETERNALLY, NEVER ENDING. UPON OUR PROPHET AND ALL OF HIS FAMILY.

Lesson 22
Tayammum

THE CONDITIONS FOR *TAYAMMUM*

There are eight conditions for *tayammum* to be correct:
1. **Niyyah**.
    <u>What is it?</u> *Niyyah* means to have a firm knowledge in the heart of what you are about to do, in this case *tayammum*.
    <u>When should it be done?</u> The *niyyah* for tayammum is done at the time of striking the hands on whatever[155] *tayammum* is performed with.

    There are three conditions for the *niyyah* to be correct:
    a) Being a Muslim,
    b) Being sane,
    c) Knowing what the *niyyah* is being made for.

    In order to perform *salah* with *tayammum* one of the following three things must be included in the *niyyah*:
    - Either the intention to achieve *tahaarah*[156],
    - or the intention to make *salah* permissible,
    - or the intention to perform any *ibaadah maqsoodah*,[157] which is not permissible without purity[158].

    If a person performs *tayammum* and his *niyyah* is just to do *tayammum*, or just to recite the Holy Qur'an (from memory), then he should not perform *salah* with this *tayammum* (providing he is not a *junubi*)[159].

2. The second condition for *tayammum* to be correct is; **the presence of a valid reason/cause that makes *tayammum* permissible**, like any of the following:
    a) Being at least one mile away from water; whether in a city, village, desert or otherwise,

---

[155] Tayammum can be performed with anything which has the same origin as the earth, (see condition 3).

[156] (الطهارة) Tahaarah means purity.

[157] (عبادة المقصودة) Ibaadah maqsoodah is that worship for which the initial intention is made and which cannot be done without purity; for example when one performs wudhu with the intention of praying salah, then although both acts are ibaadah, but wudhu is ghair-maqsoodah (i.e. not intended initially) and a step for reaching the intended worship, which is salah. Another example would be if someone did tayammum with the intention of just touching the Holy Qur'an, he cannot pray salah with this tayammum because touching the Holy Qur'an is also not an ibaadah maqsoodah.

[158] Which is not permissible without purity means that if someone did tayammum in order to do something for which wudhu is not fardh, but is mustahab, like learning Islamic knowledge, answering the adhaan or narrating a hadith, then he cannot pray salah with this tayammum.

[159] If tayammum is done by a junubi, with the niyyah of tahaarah, for example, then he may perform with that tayammum any ibaadah he wishes, like salah, touching the Qur'an etc.

b) The presence of such an illness that if water is used the illness will become worse or prolonged,

c) Such severe cold that there is fear of losing a body part if washed with water (e.g. through frostbite),

d) If there is fear of being attacked by an enemy[160],

e) Fear of thirst if water is limited, or if the water present is needed for making dough- for bread, but not for making curry[161],

f) The absence of a tool, with which to remove water from a well etc. such as a rope and bucket,

g) If there is fear of missing *Salah-tul-Janazah* or *Salah-tul-Eid*, even if these are prayed as *bina*.[162] The fear of missing *Salah-tul-Jumu'ah* and the five daily prayers is not a valid excuse[163].

3. Third, **to perform *tayammum* with something *taahir* which has the same origin as the earth**[164], such as soil, stone, and sand; but not wood, silver or gold[165].

4. **To cover the whole area** of *tayammum* (which is the face and arms) **with *mas'h***.

5. **To perform *mas'h* with the whole hand**, or most of it. If *mas'h* is done with two fingers, this is not allowed, even if you repeat it again and again until the whole area is covered. The opposite is true for *mas'h* of the head in *wudhu*.[166]

6. **To strike the ground** (or that thing with which *tayammum* is being performed) **twice with the palms of both hands**, even if it is in one place. If the body (of a traveller, for example) is covered with dust and he performs *mas'h* on it with the *niyyah* of *tayammum*, then this will act as the two blows on the ground.

---

[160] If it was not possible to reach a water source without danger from an enemy, it would be permissible to perform tayammum. An example of this was seen when Sayyiduna Imam Hussain ؑ prayed salah with tayammum during the Battle of Karbala, despite being so close to the River Euphrates.

[161] Bread is a necessity whereas, making curry is not, this is why if the water is needed to make bread then he may perform tayammum, however if the water is needed to make curry then he must use that water to perform wudhu and he cannot perform tayammum whilst he has access to that water.

[162] (و لو بناءً) "Even if these are prayed as bina," bina means foundation, so it means continuing a salah that was broken on the same foundation that it was began with. For example if someone was praying Salah-tul-Eid and his wudhu broke, leaving him without enough time to do wudhu and return to the jama'ah, it is permissible for him to do tayammum where he is standing and continue with the salah.

[163] This is because the five daily prayers can be prayed as qadha, and Zuhr can be prayed in place of jumu'ah. However, there is no replacement for janazah or Eid prayer.

[164] A simple test to see if something is from the origin of the earth is to see if it is burnt or melted by fire; if it is then it is from the origin of the earth, otherwise not. This rule is a general guide.

[165] Wood, silver and gold etc are not from the same origin as the earth.

[166] In wudhu if only two fingers are used for mas'h again and again until the fardh area is covered, then this is permissible. However, this is not the case in tayammum and he must use all or most of his hands to perform the mas'h.

7. **That those things that are against *tayammum*** (and *tahaarah*) such as *haidh*, *nifaas* and *hadath* **have stopped**.

8. **The absence of those things that stop *mas'h***, such as wax and fat.

The purpose of *tayammum*, and the conditions that make it *wajib* are the same as those already stated for *wudhu*.

There are two *rukn* of *tayammum*: *mas'h* of the hands, and *mas'h* of the face.

Summary

Fill in the gaps using the words at the bottom.

Tayammum means to become pure using the _____ when you are unable to use water. There are eight conditions for tayammum.
They are:
1. _____
2. A valid _____
3. Using something _____ from the earth.
4. To do mas'h on all the _____ and arms.
5. To do _____ with the whole hand.
6. To strike the surface twice with the _____ of both hands.
7. That those things against _____ have stopped.
8. There is _____ which stops mas'h.

Tayammum will not be correct if any of these conditions are missing.

taahir   purity   niyyah   reason   earth

face   nothing   mas'h   palms

Lesson 23
Tayammum

THE *SUNAN* OF *TAYAMMUM*

There are seven *sunan* of *tayammum*:
1. To say *tasmiyyah* at the start,
2. To perform it in the prescribed order (i.e. first face, then hands),
3. To perform it continuously (without a break),
4. To move both hands forward after placing them in the dust,
5. To then move them backward,
6. To shake excess dust off the hands,
7. To keep the fingers spread apart.

SOME EXTRA INFORMATION

- It is *mustahab* to delay *tayammum* if there is hope of finding water before the time of *salah* runs out.
- It is *wajib* to delay *tayammum* if someone has made a promise of water, even if there is danger of the *salah* becoming *qadhaa*.[167]
- It is *wajib* to delay *tayammum*; if clothes[168] or tools[169] have been promised; until there is danger of *qadhaa*[170].
- It is *wajib* to seek water for a distance of 400 paces, if it is believed to be nearby, and possible to obtain without danger.
- It is *wajib* to seek water from the people in the locality if you are in a place where the people are friendly. If they say that they will only sell the water at the normal market price[171]; then you must buy it, if you have money left over from your travelling costs.

- It is permissible to perform any number of *fara'idh* and *nawaafil* with one *tayammum*[172].
- There is no harm in performing *tayammum* before *salah* time begins.

---

[167] What is meant here is that even if he begins to fear that there is so little time left for salah that if he delays it any longer he will miss the salah, he should still wait for the person who has promised to bring him water.

[168] Because covering those areas of the body which you cannot show another person is one of the conditions that must be met before praying salah.

[169] With which to obtain water, from a well for example, like rope and bucket etc.

[170] This means that he should only wait until that time when he is sure he has enough time to pray. If he begins to think that the time is running out, then in this case he should not wait any longer.

[171] Normal price means the price that is normally charged for water in that area at that time. If they try to charge him an excessive amount then he does not have to buy the water and is allowed to do tayammum instead.

[172] Tayammum is a replacement for wudhu, so just like you can pray as many salahs as you wish with one wudhu, the same is true for tayammum.

- If half or more of the body is injured then *tayammum* should be performed, and if less than half is injured then you should wash it and perform *mas'h* (with water) on the injured area.

- You should not mix washing and *tayammum*[173].

- Those things that break *wudhu* also break *tayammum*. In addition to this, the ability to use enough water also breaks *tayammum*[174].

- If somebody's hands and feet are cut off and the face is injured, he should perform *salah* without *tahaarah*, and there is no need to repeat any *salah* performed in this state.

CHECKLIST ✓✓✓

- WHAT DOES TAYAMMUM MEAN?

- WHICH SURAH(S) CONTAIN(S) THE RULING OF TAYAMMUM? WHAT ARE THE AYAH NUMBERS?

- WHICH EVENT CAUSED THESE VERSES TO BE REVEALED? IN WHICH YEAR DID THIS EVENT TAKE PLACE?

- WHAT IS THE TITLE OF THE WIVES OF RASOOLULLAH ﷺ WHICH MEANS "MOTHER OF THE BELIEVERS?"

- HOW CAN YOU TEST IF SOMETHING IS FROM THE SAME ORIGIN AS THE EARTH?

---

[173] For example, it is not correct to wash the hands and do tayammum of the face. If he is unable to use water on one part of the body, even by mas'h, then he should do tayammum on all the required parts.
[174] If enough water became available with which you can perform wudhu; or if someone was ill and couldn't use water, but then became better; or if there was danger in the way of the water and then this danger was removed etc.

TRAINING TASK

Your teacher has had to go away on urgent business. He needs to reply to some important e-mails when he returns and has asked you to prepare some draft answers to the questions. Using your knowledge of tayammum, write brief notes on the answers to the e-mails below.

Messages Requiring Attention

Name	E-mail	Subject	Question	Response
Akbar Hussain	akbar_h@asr.com	Tayammum	I performed tayammum and performed the fara'idh of Zuhr and 'Asr aswell as the sunan and nawaafil. I have been told that I should have performed separate tayammum for 'Asr so I must pray it again. Is this true?	
Amena Khan	akhan@tb.com	Tayammum	Is it true that only men are allowed to do tayammum? If so, isn't this unfair on women?	
Sajid Malik	sajmal786@journe.com	Tayammum	I am a journalist and was recently travelling through a desert area. I only had enough water present for drinking. I tried to buy some water from local people but they wanted to charge me five times the normal rate because I was a foreigner. I refused to pay and did tayammum instead, even though I had enough money to buy the water. Now my friend says that I should have bought the water and I must repeat the salah which I prayed there. What should I do?	
Sophia Qarashi	qarsh@freepal.com	Tayammum	I live in occupied Palestine. Our water supply has been cut off by Israeli bulldozers. We rely on a well which is situated half a mile away; however, a curfew has been put in place which means we cannot leave our home at certain times. Can we do tayammum if we run out of water during the curfew hours?	

Lesson 24
Mas'h

MAS'H ON *KHUFFAIN*[175] (Wiping on Leather Socks)

It is permissible to perform *mas'h* on *khuffain* in the state of *al-hadath al-asghar*[176] for men and women. These *khuffain* can be made of any dense/thick material[177], not just leather. It makes no difference if they are entirely leather or have only leather soles[178]. [See Figure 2.1]

For *mas'h* on leather socks to be correct there are seven conditions:
1. That **they are worn after washing the feet,** even if they are worn before completing *wudhu*. The condition for this is that you must complete *wudhu* before anything breaks it[179],
2. That **they cover the ankles**[180],
3. That **it is possible to walk constantly whilst wearing them**[181] (Therefore, *mas'h* is not permissible on glass, wooden or metal socks),
4. That **both of the socks are free from any tear**, which is bigger than the size of the three smallest toes[182],
5. That **they remain on the feet** without the need to be tied down with something else,
6. That **they prevent water from reaching the body**.
7. **That the front part of the foot is present**[183]. The part which is there must be at least the size of the three smallest fingers. If the toe end of the foot is cut off, it is not permissible to perform *mas'h* on leather socks even if the heel end is present.

---

[175] (الخفين) Khuffain is dual of Khuff, which means leather sock.

[176] (الحدث الاصغر) Al-hadath al-asghar means not being in wudhu, so it would not be permissible for a junubi to do mas'h on khuffain.

[177] Such as plastic, rubber etc. By thick/dense it means any material which would stop water from reaching the skin and the sock would stay above the ankle without being tied down. It is not permissible to do mas'h on normal cotton/woollen socks that allow water to seep through.

[178] This refers to the two types of khuff; the first is called mujallad,(مجلّد) this means they are made of leather from top to bottom. The second type is called muna'all,(منعّل) these are made of something other than leather on the top part but the soles are made of leather. Mas'h may be done one any of these two types, providing they fulfil all the conditions stated.

[179] For example; Ali, and Zubair washed thier feet and wore khuffain, then Ali completed the rest of his wudhu but Zubair had a nosebleed before he was able to complete his wudhu. It is okay for Ali to perform mas'h on his khuffain if he needs to do wudhu again but Zubair must remove the khuffain, and start all over again before he can wear his khuffain. Sa'd, on the other hand, completed all his wudhu first, then wore his khuffain, it is permissible for Sa'd to do mas'h on his khuffain.

[180] If you wear socks and then wear khuffain over them, you must be careful to make sure that the khuffain come over the ankles, it will not be sufficient for just the socks to cover the ankles and the khuffain to be below the ankles.

[181] You must be able to walk a few miles comfortably in them according to your normal routine.

[182] If one of the khuffain has this much of a tear in it then mas'h is not permissible. If both are torn and the combined total is this much then it is permissible.

[183] The front part of the foot, at least the size of three small fingers must be there, because this is the amount of the foot that it is fardh to perform mas'h on. If it is missing then there is nowhere to perform mas'h on, therefore, there is no mas'h. If the other foot is complete then it will not be permissible to do mas'h on one khuff and wash the other foot because you cannot combine washing and mas'h.

Figure 2.1

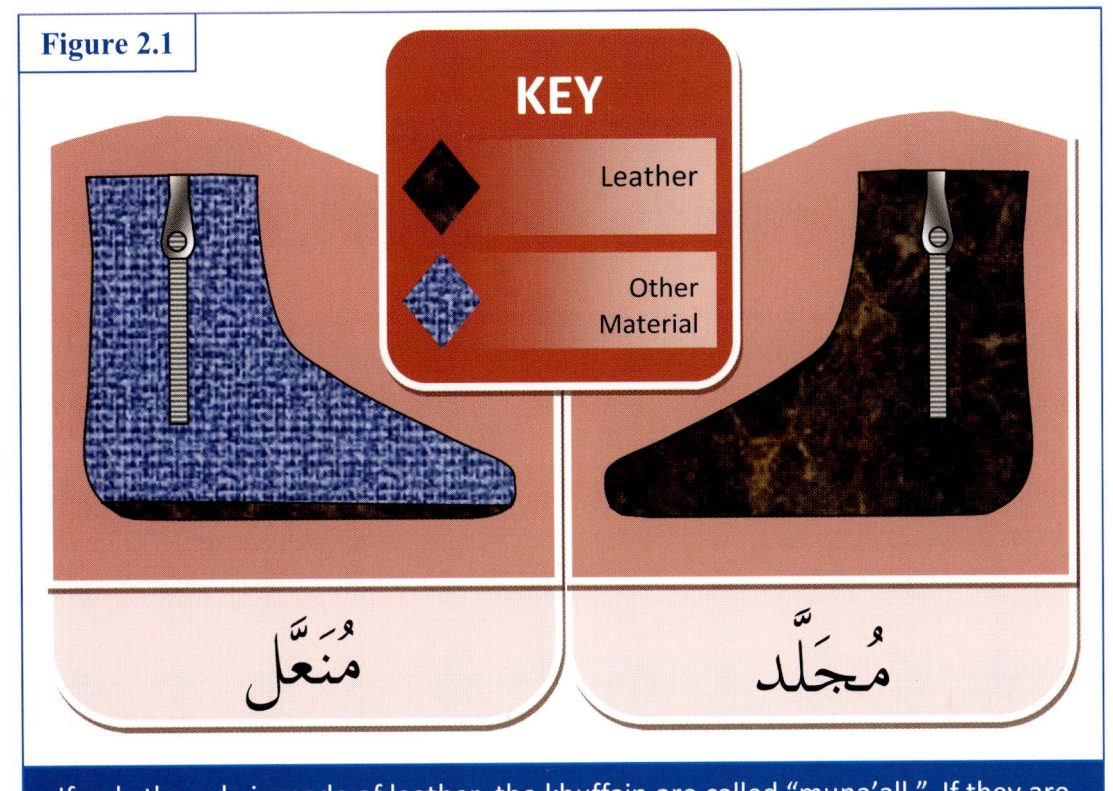

| مُنَعَّل | مُجَلَّد |

If only the sole is made of leather, the khuffain are called "muna'all." If they are made of leather entirely, then they are called "mujallad."

A *muqeem*[184] can perform *mas'h* on leather socks for up to one day and one night and a *musaafir*[185] may perform *mas'h* for up to three days and three nights. The beginning of this *mas'h* period is the first time *hadath* occurs after wearing the *khuffain*.

If a *muqeem* performed *mas'h* on his *khuffain* and then became a *musaafir* before the end of the *mas'h* period then he may complete the period of a *musaafir*.

If a *musaafir* became a *muqeem* after performing *mas'h* for one day and night then he must remove the *khuffain* and wash the feet, otherwise he may complete one day and night.

It is *fardh* to perform *mas'h* on an area at least the size of three fingers, based on the little finger, on the top part of the front of both feet. The *sunnah* way is to run the fingers from the top of the toes towards the shins, whilst keeping the fingers spread apart. [See Figure 2.2]

---

[184] (مقيم) Muqeem means a resident.

[185] (مسافر) Musaafir means a traveller. In shariah terms, a musaafir is someone who has left home with the intention of travelling to a distance which a camel travels at a medium pace, in 3 days and nights whilst travelling during the day and resting at night. The modern scholars have equated this to be equivalent to approximately 100 kilometres (62.14 miles).

Figure 2.2

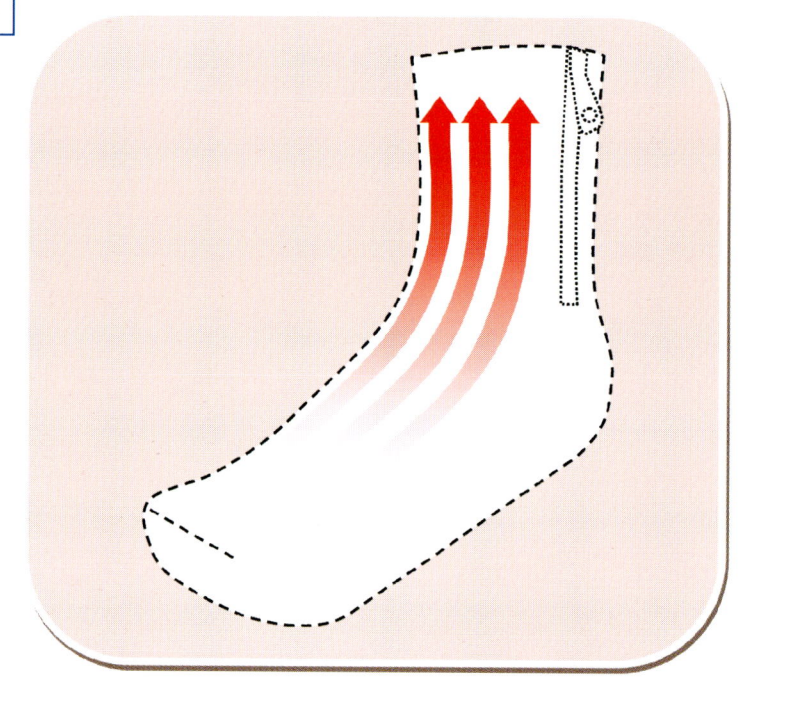

The sunnah way of wiping over leather socks is to run the wet fingers over the top of both socks starting from the toes going towards the shins whilst having the fingers spaced apart.

Four things break the *mas'h* of *khuffain*:
1. **All the things that break *wudhu***.
2. **If the leather sock is taken off**, or if most of the foot comes out of it from the shin end of the sock.
3. **If water reaches most of any foot** inside the socks[186].
4. **When the *mas'h* period ends**, except if there is fear of damaging the foot due to severe cold[187].

In the case of 2, 3 and 4 it is permissible to just wash the feet rather than doing *wudhu* all over again.

It is not permissible to do *mas'h* on:
- a turban,
- a hat,
- a *burqu'*[188],
- gloves.

---

[186] This is an authentic ruling.
[187] This means that if the weather is so cold that a person fears that his feet will become damaged by the severe cold if he takes his khuffain off to wash his feet then he may continue to do mas'h on then until he is able to remove them safely.
[188] (برقع) A burqu' (burkah) is a garment worn by pious Muslim women to cover their bodies when they go out of their homes. It is also known as jilbab or abayah.

Lesson 25
Mas'h

MAS'H ON BANDAGES

If someone had cupping done, or injured or broke any part of the body; and then had a bandage or a cast placed upon it so that he was unable to wash that part or to perform *mas'h* on it, then it is *wajib* for him to perform *mas'h* on most of the bandage/cast.

In the case of cupping (blood letting) it is enough to just perform *mas'h* over the skin that is visible between the bandages[189].

Mas'h on bandages is as if that part has been washed, so there is no time limit placed on it like there is for *mas'h* on *khuffain*.

It is not necessary for the bandage to have been put on whilst in a state of *tahaarah*.

It is permissible to wash one foot whilst having performed *mas'h* on a bandage on the other foot[190].

If the bandage falls off before the wound has healed the *mas'h* does not break[191]. It is also permissible to change one bandage with another one, and it is not *wajib* to re-do *mas'h* on the second bandage, although it is preferred.

When a doctor has advised someone not to wash the eye due to an illness, or someone's nail is broken and he has placed medication[192] on it, which is painful or damaging to remove then *mas'h* is permissible. If even *mas'h* is painful or damaging then he should leave it.

Niyyah is not necessary for the *mas'h* of *khuffain*, bandages or the head[193].

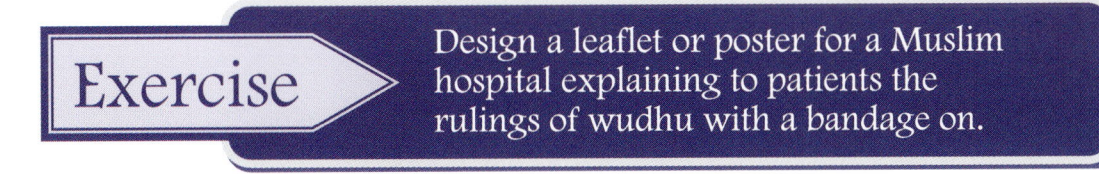

Exercise: Design a leaflet or poster for a Muslim hospital explaining to patients the rulings of wudhu with a bandage on.

---

[189] It could be that several small bandages are placed which do not cover a large area, in this case it is sufficient to do mas'h on the areas of skin that are visible between the bandages.
[190] Because mas'h is in place of washing so it is as if both feet have been washed.
[191] If the bandage falls off and the wound has healed then it is fardh to wash that part.
[192] This can be in the form of a glue-like gum or some traditional healers recommend the skin of gall-bladder.
[193] This is because mas'h is in place of washing and washing is a part of wudhu and niyyah is not fardh in wudhu.

Lesson 26
Haidh, Nifaas & Istihaadhah

DEFINING *HAIDH, NIFAAS & ISTIHAADHAH*

- Three types of blood is discharged from a woman's private part[194]:
    1. *Haidh*
    2. *Nifaas*
    3. *Istihaadhah*

- **Haidh** is the monthly blood that is discharged by the womb of a healthy[195], adult[196] female, who is not pregnant[197] and who has not reached the age of menopause[198].
- The minimum duration of *haidh* is three days, the average is five and the maximum is ten days.

- **Nifaas** is the blood discharged by the womb of a woman just after childbirth.
- The maximum duration of *nifaas* is forty days and there is no minimum[199].

- **Istihaadhah** is that blood, the duration of which is less than three days or more than ten[200] during *haidh* and greater than forty in the case of *nifaas*.[201]

- The minimum duration of purity between two periods of *haidh* is fifteen days[202] and there is no limit on its maximum[203]...

    (...EXCEPT for that woman who became an adult whilst in the state of *istihaadhah*[204]).

---

[194] This means that three types of blood exits a woman's body through her private parts although it is only haidh and nifaas that originate from the womb.
[195] Healthy: This means that she does not have an illness related to her womb which causes her to bleed from her private parts. So a woman who was suffering from an illness which is not related to her womb would still be considered healthy in this context.
[196] In the eyes of the Shariah, a woman is considered to be an adult when her periods begin, this is typically from the age of nine upwards but can be lower.
[197] Haidh stops during pregnancy; this is why missing a period is seen as one of the earliest indications of pregnancy. Therefore any bleeding during pregnancy is not haidh, it is istihaadhah.
[198] Menopause is that age in a woman's life when she stops ovulating and therefore haidh stops.
[199] Because it is possible for a woman to give birth and not bleed at all. If this is the case then her wudhu would be broken, and ghusl would be mustahab, not fardh.
[200] If she has a norm (عادة معروفة) of seven days, for example, and her haidh goes over ten days, then anything after seven days is all said to be istihaadhah.
[201] Also, any bleeding outside of haidh and nifaas (during purity) will also be istihaadhah.
[202] A woman's monthly cycle can be between twenty-five and thirty days. If her cycle is twenty-five days and she has a period of ten days then this will leave fifteen days of purity between her two cycles.
[203] This is because it is possible for haidh to stop due to certain illnesses such as the shortage of blood in the body etc. In this case it is possible for a woman not to have her period for months or even years.

	Haidh	Nifaas	Istihaadhah
What does it mean?			
Who does it affect?			
When does it occur?			
How long does it last?			
Where does it originate from?			

> **THINK…**
>
> There are many belief systems and ways of life in the world. Islam is the way of life which complements the nature on which people are created. Here is a comparison between the three major religions in the world to illustrate this point.
>
> In the Jewish faith when women are menstruating they must live, eat and sleep separately to their family. They may be confined to special quarters and can only re-join their families when the bleeding stops.
>
> In the Christian faith the opposite is true and no restrictions are placed on the women during this time. She may even sleep with her partner at this time.
>
> The Muslim way of life strikes the perfect balance and says that a man must not have intercourse with his wife during this time because it is damaging to her health and his, but she may live, eat and interact with the family as normal in every other way.
>
> [Tafseer Zia-ul-Qur'an – Justice Pir Muhammad Karam Shah رحمه الله]

---

[204] This means that if a woman was bleeding constantly at the time that she became an adult then we don't know what her normal days of haidh are due to the continual blood. So the scholars have ordained that her haidh will be ten days at the beginning of every lunar month and her nifaas will be forty days. Because a lunar month has twenty-nine or thirty days, ten of which must be counted as haidh, this leaves nineteen or twenty days of purity. This will mean that the minimum days of purity for a mustahaadhah in every month are nineteen and the maximum are twenty.

Lesson 27
Haidh – Nifaas – Istihaadhah

THE EFFECTS OF *HAIDH, NIFAAS* & *ISTIHAADHAH*

- Eight things become *haram* with *haidh* and *nifaas*:
    1. *Salah*,
    2. Fasting,
    3. Reciting (even one *ayah* of) the Holy Qur'an,
    4. Touching the Qur'an (except with a thick *ghilaaf*[205]),
    5. Entering the *masjid*,
    6. Performing *tawaaf* of the Holy Ka'bah,
    7. Sexual intercourse,
    8. Taking benefit from the area between the navel and the knees[206].

- If the blood stops at the end of the maximum duration of *haidh* or *nifaas* then intercourse becomes permissible without performing *ghusl*[207].

- If the blood stops before the maximum period, according to her normal routine, then intercourse is not permissible until:
    - Either she performs *ghusl*,
    - Or she performs *tayammum*,
    - Or *salah* becomes a debt upon her[208].

- A *haa-idh*[209] and *nufasaa*[210] will perform *qadhaa* of any fasts missed and not of any *salah* missed.

- Five things become *haram* with *janabah*:
    1. *Salah*,
    2. Reciting (even one *ayah* from) the Qur'an,
    3. Touching the Qur'an (except with a thick *ghilaaf*),
    4. Entering the *masjid*,
    5. Performing *tawaaf* of the Holy Ka'bah.

---

[205] (الغلاف المتجافي) Thick ghilaaf: A covering made out of some thick material that is separate from the actual book, so that the book is removed or separated from it when recited.

[206] This means that not only is intercourse haram during these days, but her husband cannot even touch the area between the navel and the knees for purposes of pleasure; so, for example, using her thighs for pleasure is also not allowed during this time.

[207] Although it is much better to perform ghusl first.

[208] For example, if the blood stopped during Zuhr time, and there is enough time remaining until the beginning of 'Asr time for her to do ghusl and say the tahreemah (الله اكبر), or a little more time than that, but she does not perform ghusl, (or in the absence of water, she does not do tayammum) until the time for Zuhr finishes. Zuhr salah has now become a debt upon her and she must perform its qadhaa.

[209] (الحائض) A haa-idh is a woman in the state of haidh.

[210] (النّفساء) A nufasaa is a woman in nifaas.

- Three things become *haram* upon a *muhdith*[211]:
    1. *Salah*,
    2. *Tawaaf* of the Holy *Ka'bah*,
    3. Touching the *Qur'an* (except with a thick *ghilaaf*).

- The blood of a *mustahaadhah*[212] is like a continuous nosebleed. It doesn't stop *salah*, fasting and intercourse.

- A *mustahaadhah* or someone with an *'uzr* (illness) such as continuous urine drops, or continuous release of wind etc, should perform *wudhu* at the beginning of the time for each *fardh salah*.

- He/She may perform with this *wudhu* whatever he/she wishes from *fara'idh* and *nawaafil*.

- The *wudhu* of these *ma'zoor*[213] persons is only broken by the time of that *fardh salah* finishing.

- The *shariah* does not recognise anyone as a *ma'zoor* until the *'uzr*[214] does not encompass the entire time for one *fardh salah* in such a way that the *'uzr* doesn't even stop for that amount of time in which it is possible to perform *wudhu* and *salah*[215]. This is the condition for someone to be proven as a *ma'zoor*.

- The condition for someone to remain as a *ma'zoor* is that the *'uzr* remains during the whole time after it has been proven. Even if this *'uzr* occurs just once in each *salah* time.

- The condition for the ending of that *'uzr* and for that person to no longer remain a *ma'zoor* is that the complete time for one *fardh salah* passes without this *'uzr* re-occurring.

---

[211] (المحدث) A muhdith is a person in the state of al-hadath al-asghar

[212] (المستحاضة) A mustahaadhah is a woman who has istihaadhah.

[213] (معذور) A ma'zoor is that person whom the shariah recognizes as having a valid reason as a result of which he cannot keep his wudhu.

[214] (عذر) 'Uzr means illness, reason, or excuse.

[215] Approximately 15-20 minutes depending on how long it takes someone to perform wudhu and salah.

ACTIVITY ONE

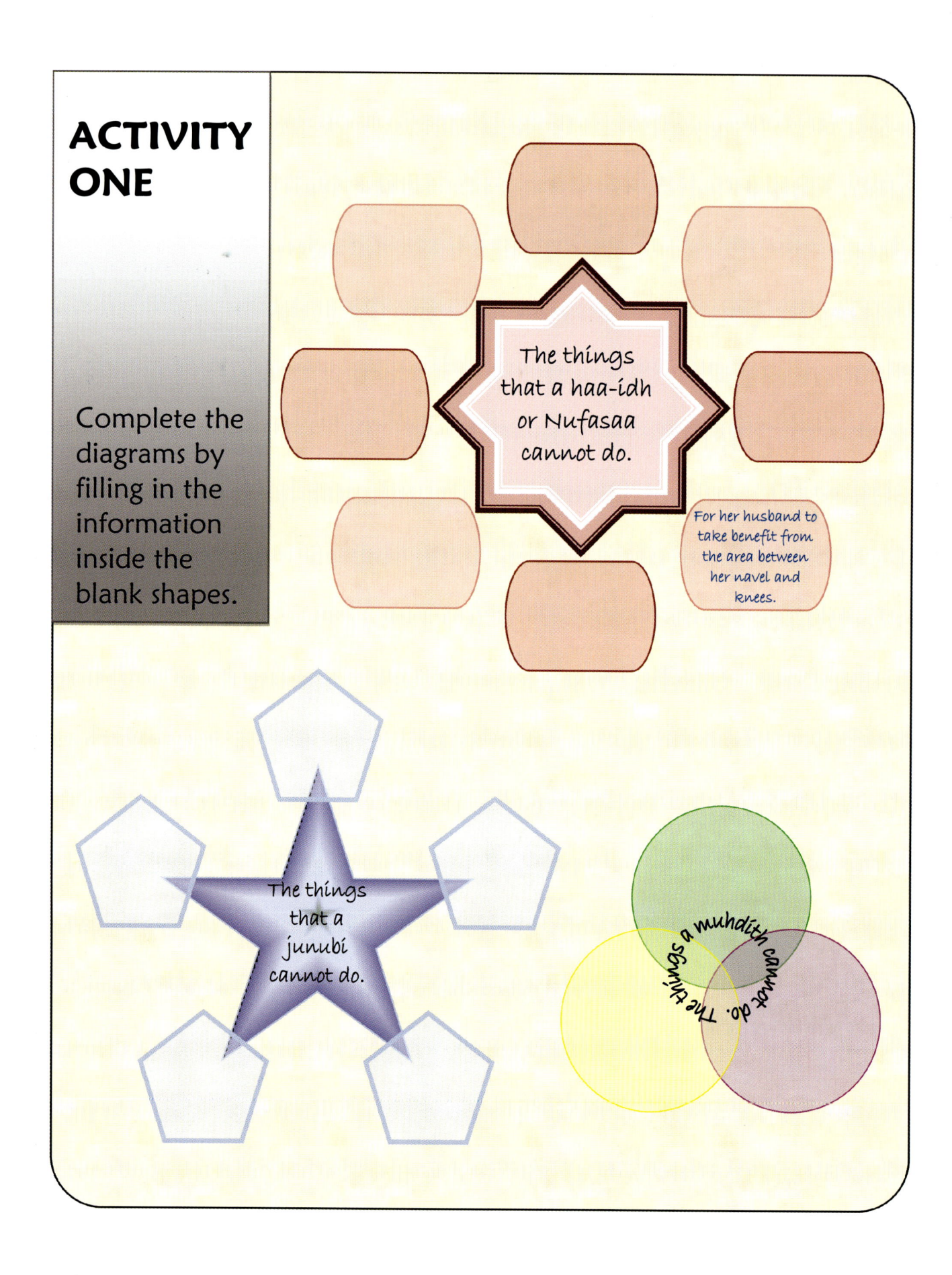

Complete the diagrams by filling in the information inside the blank shapes.

The things that a haa-idh or Nufasaa cannot do.

For her husband to take benefit from the area between her navel and knees.

The things that a junubi cannot do.

The things a muhdith cannot do.

58

ACTIVITY TWO

Dr Abdul Hakeem's secretary has accidently mixed up yesterday's patient records. File the records shown overleaf into the correct filing cabinet depending on whether the patient is ma'zoor or not.

Ma'zoor

Non Ma'zoor

59

NOTE: For stickers, see the 'Sticker Section' at the back of this book

INSTRUCTIONS FOR ACTIVITY TWO

Here are the records that need to be filed. Peel each one off and sort out the ma'zoor patients from the non-ma'zoor ones. Now stick one record in each level of the correct filing cabinet taking care that the surnames are filed in alphabetical order.

Mrs S Hussain
Flu

Mr L Khan
Constant nosebleed

Mrs K Tabassum
Urine drops every 2-3 hours

Mr A Tahir
Non-stop wind

Miss Z Khatun
Infected wound, non-stop discharge of pus

Mr F Islam
Swollen ankles

Mr L Iqbal
Weak bladder - 1 urine drop every 5 minutes.

Mrs Y Alawiah
Consant bleeding (istihaadhah)

Ms N Ayn
Broken arm

Mr M Javed
Back pain

Lesson 28
Anjaas

THE TYPES OF *ANJAAS*[216] (Impurities)

There are two types of *haqeeqiyyah najasah*:
1. *Ghaleezah*[217],
2. *Khafeefah*[218].

Examples of *ghaleezah*:
a. Alcohol,
b. Flowing[219] blood,
c. The meat or hide (skin) of *al-maytah*[220],
d. The urine of those animals whose meat is not eaten[221],
e. The excrement of dogs,
f. The excrement and saliva of predatory animals,
g. The excrement of chickens, ducks, and geese,
h. All those things that break the *wudhu* if they are discharged from a person's body.

Examples of *Khafeefah*:
a. The urine of horses,
b. The urine of *halal* animals,
c. The excrement of *haram* birds.

- Up to the area of one *dirham*[222] is forgiven in *ghaleezah*.

- Up to a quarter of the clothes and a quarter of the body is forgiven in the case of *khafeefah*.

- The splashes of urine which are the size of the head of a needle are also forgiven.

---

[216] (أنجاس) Anjaas is plural of (نجاسة) najasah, which means, dirt/filth/impurity. Najasah is of two types (حقيقية) haqeeqiyyah, and (حكمية) hukmiyyah. Najasah haqeeqiyyah is actual impurity like alcohol. Najasah hukmiyyah is that which comes under the ruling of impurity, like a junubi, and has been dealt with in previous chapters, such as haidh, nifaas and hadath etc. This topic is now concerning haqeeqiyyah (actual) impurity.

[217] (الغليظة) Extremely impure. This is that najaasah, in which there is no doubt about its impurity. All the scholars agree that it is impure.

[218] (الخفيفة) Less impure. There is some disagreement between the scholars in this type.

[219] Circulating.

[220] (الميتة) Al-maytah means "dead". In other words, any animal which died of some cause, other than being slaughtered in accordance with the laws of shariah. Note that the hide of al-maytah is najas before being treated and becomes taahir after tanning (the process by which animal hide is converted into leather. See lesson 26).

[221] This means those animals that are not halal and therefore, Muslims do not eat their meat.

[222] A circle of approximately 1 inch diameter.

- If some *najas* bedding or *najas* earth becomes wet because of the perspiration of the person sleeping on it, or because of wetness on the feet, and the effect[223] of the *najasah* becomes apparent on the body or the feet, then they will become impure. If the effect does not show then the body/feet will not become impure.

- If a *taahir*, dry cloth was wrapped inside a damp, *najas* cloth, whose wetness does not drip if the cloth is squeezed, then this dry cloth will not become *najas*.

- If a wet cloth is spread over some dry, *najas* ground and the ground is moistened by it, then this cloth will not become *najas*.

- If a breeze blows over a *najasah* and then blows onto a cloth, this cloth will not become *najas* unless the effect of the *najasah* appears on it.

TRUE OR FALSE?

1. الخفيفة means 'extremely impure'.
2. Najasah is of two types.
3. The urine of horses is considered 'lesser impurity'.
4. If a cloth was stained with alcohol and the najasah is more than one dirham, a person can still pray in this cloth.
5. The excrement of dogs is ghaleezah.
6. If a person prayed with extremely tiny splashes of urine on his/her clothes, the salah would be valid.
7. The saliva of a cheetah is extremely impure

If anything is false write out the correct statement below.

_____
_____
_____
_____

---

[223] (الأثر) Effect means smell, taste or colour.

Lesson 29
Anjaas

HOW TO REMOVE *ANJAAS*

- If something becomes *najas* because of *najasah mariyyah*[224], it can be purified by simply removing the actual *najasah* (even if it is removed by just washing once). There is no harm if a stain is left which is difficult to remove[225].

- If the *najasah* is *ghair-mariyyah* then it can be removed by washing three times and rinsing each time. [See Figure 3.1]

- *Najasah* may be removed from the clothes or the body using water or any other liquid which is able to remove the *najasah*, such as vinegar or rose-water.

- *Najasah* may be removed from a *khuff* by rubbing with earth if the *najasah* has a body, even if it is moist[226].

- Items such as a sword[227] may be purified by simply wiping.

- If the effect[228] of a *najasah* disappears from the ground and it dries up, it is permissible to pray *salah* upon that earth but *tayammum* is not allowed with it[229]. Any trees and grass, which are standing on this ground, are also purified when it dries up.

- If the nature[230] of a *najasah* changes, for example, if it becomes salt, or if it is burnt by fire, then it no longer remains *najas*.

- Dry *mani* can be removed from the clothes or the body by scrubbing/scraping it off. If it is wet then it must be washed off to purify the body or clothes.

---

[224] In the last lesson we divided najasah into two types: haqeeqiyyah, if it is physical impurity, and hukmiyyah, if it is a state of impurity. We then divided haqeeqiyyah impurity into two types, ghaleezah and khafeefah. Here we will divide each of these into two further types:
   a) (مرئيّة) Mariyyah: visible impurity.
   b) (غير مرئيّة) Ghair-Mariyyah: non-visible impurity.

[225] For example, blood may leave a stain behind if it stains white clothes even after washing it off.
[226] What this means is that any najasah which is not thin and liquid-like, can be removed by rubbing against the earth, even if the najasah is moist (for example horse manure) because the khuff is waterproof and the najasah will not get inside its fibres.
[227] All those items which are solid and non-porous, so that the najasah stays only on the surface, such as a mirror or window pane etc. may be purified in this way.
[228] (الأثر) Effect means smell and colour etc.
[229] This is because amongst the conditions of salah is that the ground is taahir (pure), but the condition in tayammum is that the ground is mutahhir (purifying).
[230] Nature means its chemical composition

Figure 3.1

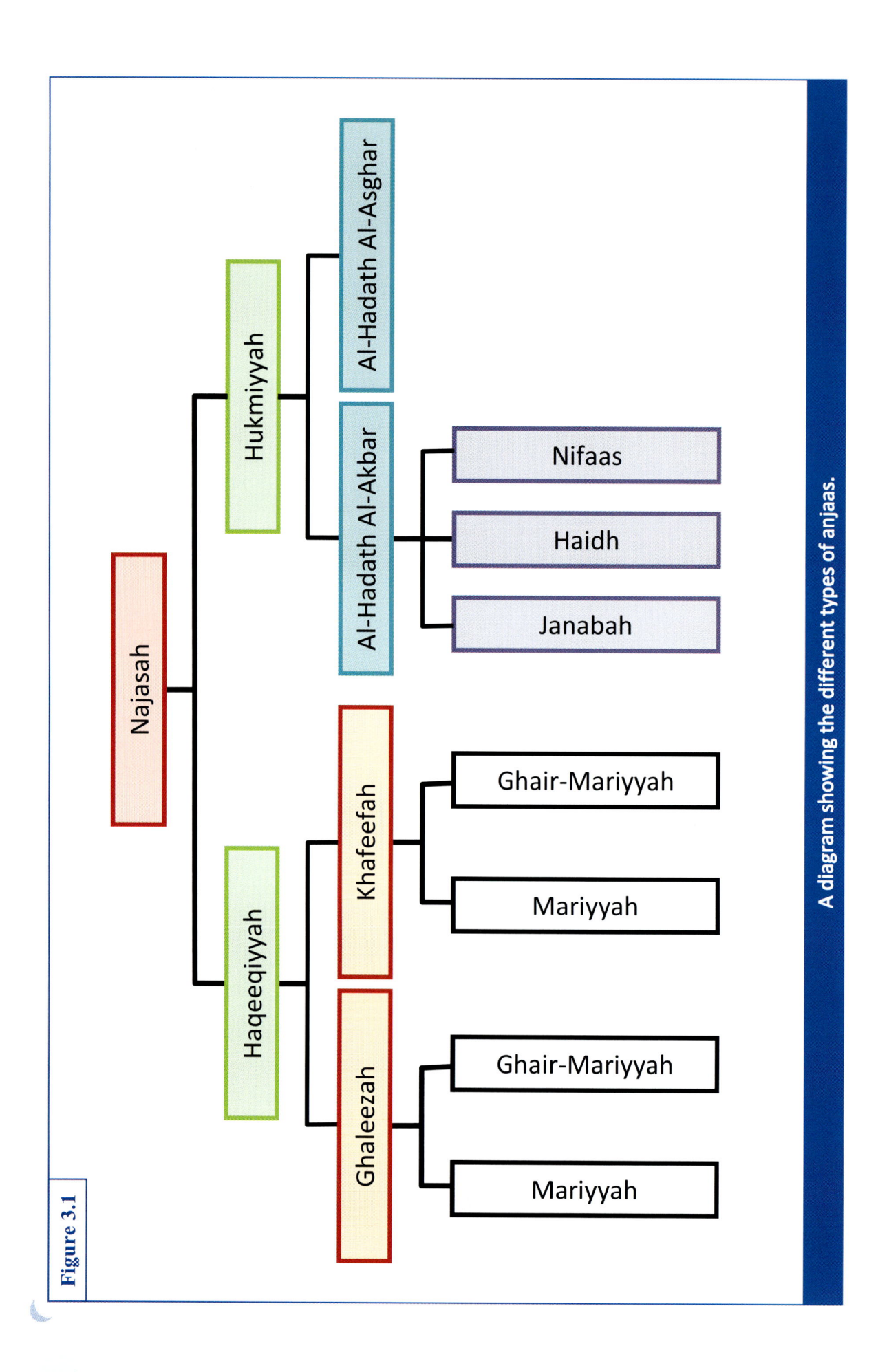

```
Najasah
├── Hukmiyyah
│   ├── Al-Hadath Al-Asghar
│   └── Al-Hadath Al-Akbar
│       ├── Nifaas
│       ├── Haidh
│       └── Janabah
└── Haqeeqiyyah
    ├── Khafeefah
    │   ├── Ghair-Mariyyah
    │   └── Mariyyah
    └── Ghaleezah
        ├── Ghair-Mariyyah
        └── Mariyyah
```

A diagram showing the different types of anjaas.

64

Identify the najasah on the following things and then describe how to purify them.

Item in need of cleansing	Name & type of najasah	Method of purification
A mirror with blood on it.	Blood - mariyyah	Wipe it clean
A piece of clothing with dry mani on it.		
A prayer mat with a child's dried urine on it.		
A person slept on a hotel bed which had traces of alcohol on it. In the morning his body smelt of alcohol.		
A khuff with cat faeces on it.		
Wet mani on the body.		
The dried saliva of a dog on a dinner-plate.		
Traces of human excrement on the clothes.		
A silver ring with blood on it.		

Lesson 30
Anjaas

THE PURITY OF HIDE AND BONE

- The hide of *al-maytah*[231] is purified by tanning (دِبَاغَة [232]), whether this is done chemically, or by scrubbing with sand or drying in the sun[233], except the hide of swine and the skin of humans[234].

- The hide of all those animals that are not *halal* to eat is purified by slaughtering them according to the rules of *Shariah*, but the meat is not purified[235].

- All those things which do not contain flowing blood in them do not become *najas* with death, such as hair, feathers, hooves and bone, so long as it doesn't have fat on it. Sinews and tendons[236] are *najas* according to *sahih* narrations.

- The *naafijah-tul-misk*[237] of deer is *taahir* like the musk contained in it is *taahir*, and it is *halal* to eat.

- *Az-zabaad*[238] is *taahir* and it is permissible to perform *salah* whilst wearing this perfume.

---

[231] Any animal that has not been slaughtered in the proper way described by the Shariah, but has died of another cause, is called al-maytah.

[232] (الدباغة) Dibaaghah: Tanning. There are two types of dibaaghah, (حقيقية) haqeeqiyyah and (حكمية) hukmiyyah. Dibaaghah haqeeqiyyah is actual tanning, and dibaaghah hukmiyyah is that process which carries the same ruling as actual dibaaghah.

[233] Tanning is the process by which animal hide is turned into leather. It usually involves soaking in tannic acid. Other traditional methods include scrubbing the hide with salt and sand or simply leaving the hide out in the sun to dry naturally.

[234] The hide of swine will not be purified because swine is najas al-'ayn (نجس العين). We should see that the leather products we buy, such as shoes don't contain any pig leather in them, because if they do then they are haram to wear. The skin of humans will not be purified because human beings are the best of Allah's creation and should be treated with respect, whether Muslim or non-Muslim.

[235] This is the ruling based on the most sahih narrations, this is also what the fatwa is given on.

[236] You can identify sinew by the shiny white/silvery strands you see attached to the meat when it is prepared for cooking. Tendons are made of a white rubbery material; they connect bone to muscle, for example the Achilles tendon which is the thin, tall tough part that you can feel at the bottom of your calf just above your heel. These are easily recognised because they are very tough and difficult to cut with a sharp knife, let alone chew or eat. Sinew is commonly used for making tough rope and string, like bowstring for example.

[237] (نافجة المسك) This is a special compartment in the navel of deer in which a perfume called musk is contained.

[238] (الزّباد) A strong musky perfume obtained from civets. A civet is a slender nocturnal cat with a barred and spotted coat, native to Africa and Asia.

NOTE: For stickers, see the 'Sticker Section' at the back of this book

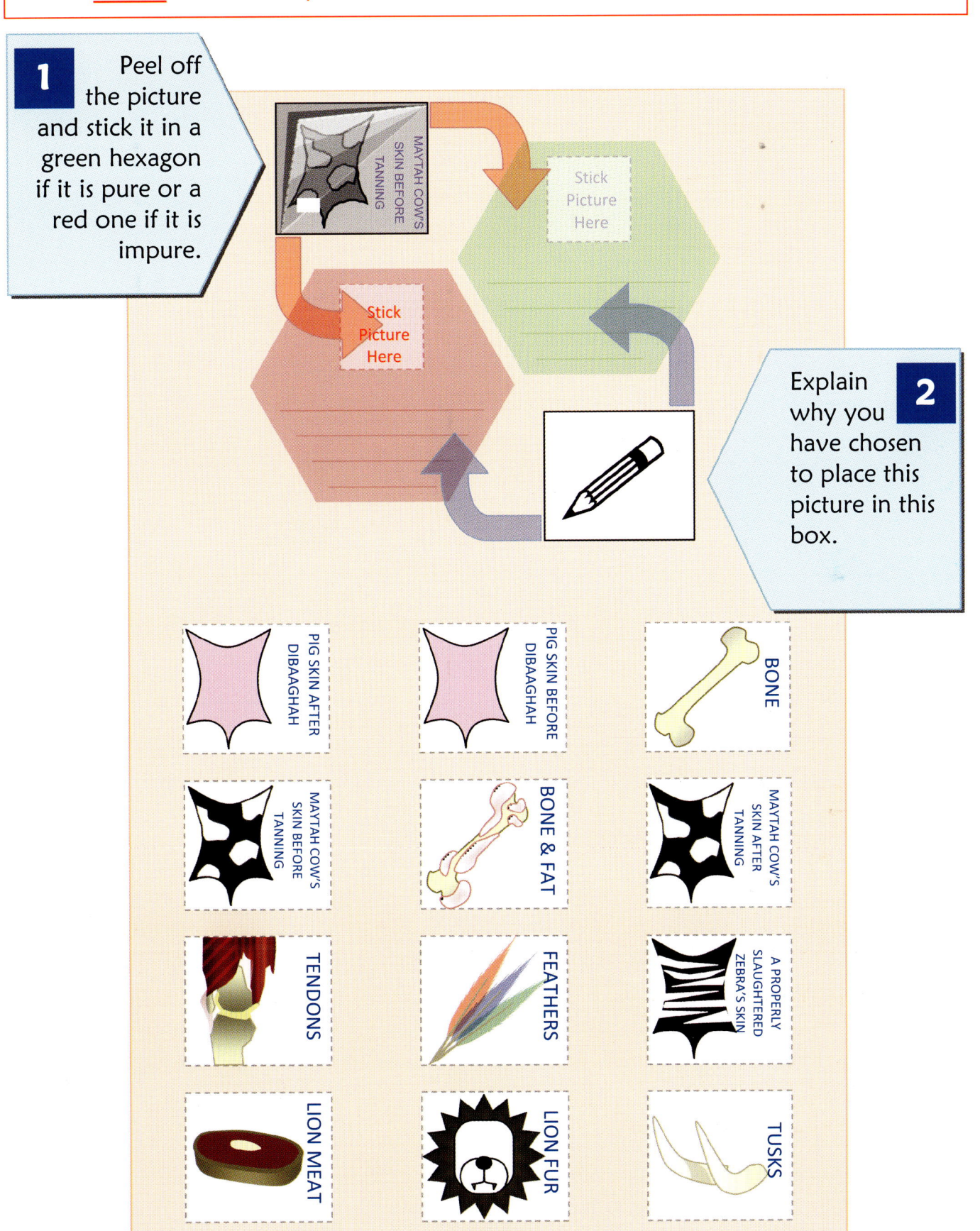

1 Peel off the picture and stick it in a green hexagon if it is pure or a red one if it is impure.

MAYTAH COW'S SKIN BEFORE TANNING

Stick Picture Here

Stick Picture Here

2 Explain why you have chosen to place this picture in this box.

- PIG SKIN AFTER DIBAAGHAH
- PIG SKIN BEFORE DIBAAGHAH
- BONE
- MAYTAH COW'S SKIN BEFORE TANNING
- BONE & FAT
- MAYTAH COW'S SKIN AFTER TANNING
- TENDONS
- FEATHERS
- A PROPERLY SLAUGHTERED ZEBRA'S SKIN
- LION MEAT
- LION FUR
- TUSKS

67

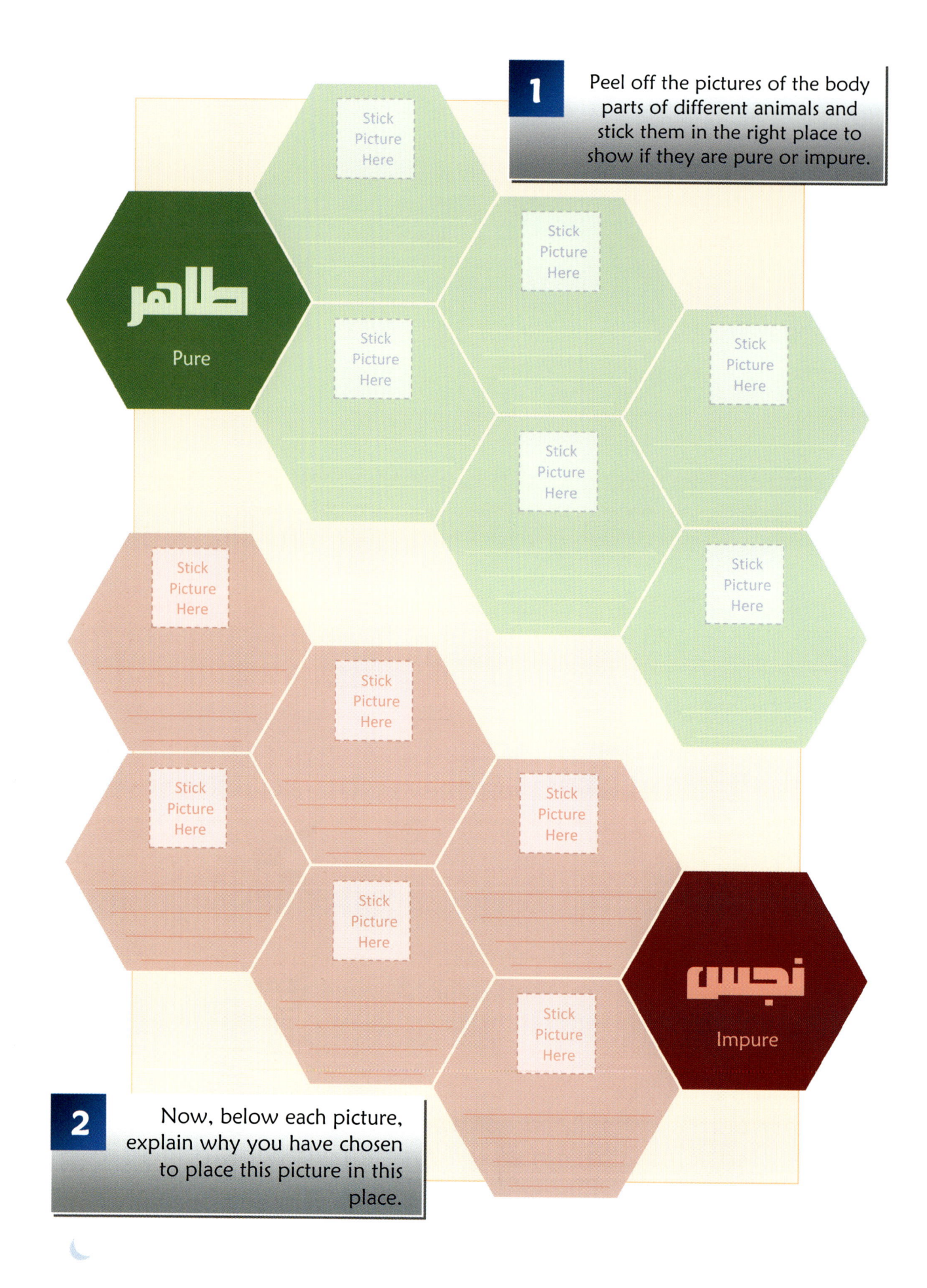

1 Peel off the pictures of the body parts of different animals and stick them in the right place to show if they are pure or impure.

طاهر
Pure

نجس
Impure

2 Now, below each picture, explain why you have chosen to place this picture in this place.

Lesson 31
Personal Hygiene, Health & Beauty

10 THINGS WHICH PROMOTE HYGIENE

The *hadith* below outlines ten things which are from the practice of the *fitrah* of a human being. *Fitrah* means 'the natural state' or those things which were practiced by the Messengers and Prophets before us to maintain cleanliness of the body and personal hygiene.

عَنْ عَائِشَةَ ﷺ قَالَتْ قَالَ رَسُوْلُ اللهِ ﷺ عَشْرٌ مِنَ الْفِطْرَةِ :
قَصُّ الشَّارِبِ وَ إِعْفَاءُ اللِّحْيَةِ وَالسِّوَاكُ وَ اسْتِنْشَاقُ الْمَآءِ وَ قَصُّ الْأَظْفَارِ وَ غَسْلُ الْبَرَاجِمِ وَ نَتْفُ الْاِبِطِ وَ حَلْقُ الْعَانَةِ وَ انْتِقَاصُ الْمَآءِ يَعْنِيْ الْاِسْتِنْجَاءَ. قَالَ الرَّاوِى وَ نَسِيْتُ الْعَاشِرَةَ اِلَّا اَنْ تَكُوْنَ الْمَضْمَضَةَ
(مُسْلِم)

It is narrated from Sayyidah 'Aisha ﷺ that that the Messenger of Allah ﷺ said 10 things are from the nature of a human:
Trimming the moustache
Leaving the beard to grow
Brushing the teeth
Cleansing the nose with water
Cutting the nails
Washing the joints of the fingers
Removing the hair from the arm-pits
Removing hair from the private parts
Washing the private parts with water after going to the toilet
The narrator says that he forgot what the tenth thing was, but it could have been rinsing the mouth with water.
(Recorded in Muslim Shareef)

THE LESSONS WE CAN LEARN FROM THIS *HADITH*

There is a lot of wisdom in the acts that are mentioned in the *hadith* and if we analyse each one of the practices mentioned we can see how acting on them can assist in maintaining health and hygiene.

Trimming the moustache: it is important to trim the moustache when it reaches such a length that the redness of the upper lip is no longer visible. The reason for this is that if the moustache is on the upper lip it is very likely that any food and drink which the person has will get caught in the hair of the moustache. This could cause a bad smell to come from the person and may also encourage the growth of bacteria on the skin under the moustache. It also looks very untidy to keep a long moustache which reaches over the upper lip, and Islam encourages us to look presentable in gatherings.

It has been said by the scholars that it is *makrooh* to shave the moustache off completely and that it is wrong to let it grow excessively, except in times of war.

Letting the beard grow: the beard should be left to grow only to the length of a fistful or four finger-lengths. This means that the hair of the beard should be graspable in one fist. It is acceptable to grow the beard more than a fistful, but it shouldn't be too long since it will look untidy, and it is considered *makrooh* to shorten the beard less than a fistful.

The beauty of a man's face is emphasised by his beard, this is why it has been the practice of all the pious men of the past, including the greatest men who were Messengers and Prophets to keep beards.

Brushing the teeth: the specific words in the *ahadith* are to use a '*miswak*', which is a stick taken from a special tree. The '*miswak*' stick has many benefits including the fact that it is *sunnah*. However the use of toothpaste and toothbrushes are an acceptable alternative.

Cleansing the teeth is a *sunnah* which has been emphasised quite a lot in other *ahadith* too. Apart from the teeth being protected from tooth-decay, gum disease and other such diseases, this practice ensures that a person has fresh breath so that people are not put off by him in social gatherings.

Washing the joints of the fingers: it is from amongst the practices of fitrah to cleanse or wash the hands, including the joints of the fingers after meals. This cleansing may be done by licking off the traces of food and washing the hands thoroughly. This cleansing will ensure that no after-smell is left on the fingers because of the food that has been eaten. It was not common practice in the days of ignorance to wash the hands after eating, and spoons etc. were not common either, so traces of food would remain in the creases of the skin, especially around the joints of the fingers. This is why it is mentioned specifically here.

Cleansing the nose with water: washing out the nostrils with water is a practice which is from the fitrah because it ensures that the filth which gathers in the nose is removed. The hairs in the nostrils have dust and dirt upon them which can cause irritation and a build-up of mucus if they are not cleansed properly. Use of a tissue is also acceptable, however because water is the primary source used for cleansing, its use is better.

Cutting the nails: it should be from amongst our weekly practices to clip the nails of our fingers and toe-nails when they grow. Much dirt and filth gathers beneath the nails, and this needs to be cleansed regularly to maintain hygiene. Obviously if we use our hands to prepare and eat food, and handle things with, then it is vital to ensure that they are clean otherwise we could be the cause of spreading disease.

Removing the pubic hair and hair from under the arm-pits: this is a practice which is often ignored or undermined by people thinking that simply washing these areas is sufficient. The hair on the private parts and under the arm-pits grows when a person attains the age of puberty, it is a sign that this person is now becoming an adult. This hair should be removed so that it is no longer visible and this is the actual *sunnah* practice.

Any appropriate method may be used to remove the hair such as shaving it with a razor, a blade, using cream or wax, or to epilate it out. It is better for the hair to be removed so that the roots are also taken out.

Doing istinjaa: the rulings on *istinjaa* and the method have been outlined in lessons 6, 7 and 8. A brief mention can be made here about the way *istinjaa* promotes hygiene by removing the filth that gathers in the private areas after relieving oneself.

In other narrations[239] a further 3 things are mentioned.

Circumcision: this practice is hygienic for the obvious reason that it allows the private part of a man to remain clean and uncontaminated from splashes of urine and the build-up of germs in that area.

Rinsing the mouth out with water: this may be done after meals, before and after sleep in order to remove food which may be stuck between the teeth and also to have breath which does not smell of foul left-over food.

---

[239] These narrations can be found in the collection of Imam At-Tirmidhi

Using perfume: this is a practice which enhances a person's interaction with others. A nice smelling person will be included more readily in social gatherings than a person who does not care to remove any body-odour using perfume.

COMPLETE THE TABLE

Fill in the blank boxes in the table showing how any ten practices mentioned above promote hygiene, health and beauty. The first row has been filled in for you.

Practice	How Does it Promote Hygiene/beauty?
Trimming the moustache	Stops food getting stuck in them and causing a smell. Also prevents build up of bacteria in them. Enhances tidiness and makes the person look presentable in public.

SOME EXTRA INFORMATION ON HYGIENE FOR WOMEN

The use of Henna and Saffron: it is considered a part of a woman's beauty to use henna and saffron on her hair, hands and body. It is also a mark of being able to distinguish between a man and woman.

Perfume: A woman is encouraged to use perfume, but only within the home. Those women who wear perfume outside their own homes have been cursed because they may become a cause of temptation by alluring people to be attracted to their nice smelling perfume.

Removing hair from the body: this is a controversial issue which needs a lot of explanation, however there are a few general guidelines which should be followed and adhered to.

Allah created human beings in the best form, and with the best shape and with intellect and understanding. It has been mentioned in the Holy Qur'an that we should not change the shape and form that He created us in. This means making permanent changes to our bodies which are not reversible, such as implants and plastic surgery. Most scholars have allowed these for medical purposes though. The reason for us not being allowed to change our original creation is that we should be happy and satisfied with what we have been given, and we should know that Allah does not judge our looks but our actions.

If the change is not permanent, then it should be noted that wasting time for beautification and adornment is not considered acceptable. So hair removal from the arms, legs and parts of the body excluding the private parts and arm-pits (because they are necessary to remove), although it is a temporary change to the creation, may be a waste of time because it will grow back, and removing it is only done for fashion purposes and not for hygiene or cleanliness.

However if a woman has excessive hair to such a degree that she is unattractive and her husband, or any future partner, feels repulsed by her looks because of this excessive hair then she has been granted permission to remove it.

Men should note however, that they have been advised to choose pious women who practice their religion, rather than those who are beautiful because physical beauty is temporary and decays over time.

Plucking eyebrows: this practice has been strictly forbidden and women who pluck their eyebrows for fashion have been cursed. However if a woman's eyesight is being obstructed then she is permitted to remove the extra hair.

END WORD

I began and I end with the name of Allah, who has no beginning and no end

All praise is for the Creator of the universe who gave us life. Endless blessings and bounties be upon our Beloved Prophet ﷺ who gave us the fiqh of living.

It is only due to the help, guidance and infinite mercy of Allah ﷻ that we have reached the end of Kitaab At-Tahaarah, the first part of this fiqh course. It is at moments like this that the following words of the Holy Qur'an spring to mind:

…and if you try to count the favours of Allah, you will not be able to… [16:18]

In another part of the Holy Qur'an Allah ﷻ says:

…and if you are grateful, I will certainly increase (my blessings upon) you… [14:7]

Allah ﷻ has blessed us with the priceless gift of knowledge; let us be sure that we are thankful for this, so that we are not listed amongst the likes of Iblees, Fir'awn and Nimrud who were favoured by Allah ﷻ but were ungrateful and turned away.

The question now is this; how do we show thanks for such an invaluable gift? I will take the support of a beautiful saying of Rasoolullah ﷺ to try to answer this question. The Messenger of Allah ﷺ said, **extend to others (the knowledge of deen) from me, even if it is one ayah.** It has also been said that knowledge lies between two jihaads (struggles). The first struggle is to gain it, and the second struggle is to act upon it.

We can show our thanks to Allah ﷻ by firstly acting upon this knowledge ourselves, and then teaching our families and friends this knowledge. If we do this then we will have accomplished the aim of this life and we will spend eternity amongst the successful ones in the gardens of Paradise.

I pray that Allah ﷻ gives us the strength to perfect our understanding and our actions. I pray that all those who read this are triumphant in their struggle for perfection. I pray especially for my parents and my teachers whose nurturing and guidance have made me capable of attempting such a noble task, and I pray for all those who have helped me in any way whatsoever with this humble effort; the best reward is with Allah ﷻ.

M N Sialvi
Thursday 9th Shawwal 1429
9th October 2008

APPENDIX A

A Short Biography of Imam Abu Hanifah

Name: Nu'man bin Thabit
Nick Name: Abu Hanifah
Title: Imam A'dham (The Greatest Imam)
Birth: Kufah, Iraq, 80 AH
Death: Baghdad, Iraq, 150AH

Imam Abu Hanifah was a devout Muslim and a very successful businessman. He was known all over for his honesty, generosity and good character. And on top of all of this he was one of the greatest and most famous scholars in all of our Islamic history. What made him so successful was the fact that he was able to balance his worship and manage his worldly matters in a way that was very pleasing to Allah. Imam Abu Hanifah would spend his nights in worship, and his days in spreading Deen through teaching and learning, and by doing this he created ease and benefit for the whole of the Muslim Ummah. So many years after the death of this great scholar, his fiqh and school of thought are still adopted by most of the Ummah.

Imam Abu Hanifah's most blessed trait is that he had the honour of visiting Sayyiduna Anas bin Malik and narrating hadith from him and other noble Companions, which earned him the privileged rank of a Taab'i. Also, his father, who was called Sayyiduna Thabit, had the honour of serving dessert to Sayyiduna Ali who then prayed for his family.

One day the Great Imam walked past Imam Sha'bii who asked him where he was going. "To the market," replied the imam, upon which Imam Sha'bii said to him, "I see signs of great knowledge and intelligence on your face but the intelligent adopt the company of scholars." After this day our beloved Imam began to attend the gatherings of the scholars.

Imam Abu Hanifah is reported to have learned from around 4000 teachers, many of them were extremely notable personalities of the time. He spent a considerable amount of time with another great scholar called Sayyiduna Hammaad.

He often saw a dream in which he saw himself digging the grave of the Holy Prophet. He reported this dream to the greatest dream interpreter of the time, Imam Ibn Sireen, who said it means, 'you will give life to dead knowledge.'

Later on in Imam A'dham's life, Yazid bin Marwan, the governor of Kufah, wanted to appoint him as the treasurer- but he refused saying that he could not sign Yazid's false decisions of murder. This angered Yazid who ordered him to be beaten with a whip. Imam Abu Hanifah bore the punishment but did not accept the post.

Then finally, the Caliph Mansoor offered him the post of a jurist (judge). Imam A'dham replied that he was not entitled to receive it. Caliph Mansoor became angry and accused him of lying. Imam A'dham ؓ replied, "If I am lying, then it is true that I am not fit to be a jurist, because a liar cannot be a jurist." Angered by this, Caliph Mansoor had him arrested and imprisoned.

Imam A'dham ؓ continued to teach in prison, but Caliph Mansoor was terrified of him and so secretly poisoned him. The Imam realised that he had been poisoned, and so he prostrated before Almighty Allah and passed away in prostration. His funeral prayer was offered six times and there were 50,000 people in the first congregation.

The plot of these evil people to get rid of the beloved Imam ؓ may have worked physically, but the spiritual and intellectual presence of the Great Imam ؓ is still found all over the world. And his teachings are very much alive hundreds of years later because of the great blessings and goodness that he accumulated throughout his life which was dedicated to his Creator. This teaches us that although we are mortals, if we establish a strong link with Allah who is 'The Ever Living,' then He will cause our mortal life to remain alive through it being remembered on tongues of other people. This is one explanation of the ayah "Remember me, I will remember you, remain thankful to me and don't be ungrateful." [Surah Al-Baqarah]

NOTE: This is a very brief account of the life of the Great Imam ؓ taken from the following sources; refer to them for more detail.

1. Manaaqib Imam A'dham – Imam Mawqif bin Ahmed Makki d.568AH
2. Al-Fiqh Al-Hanafi Wa Addillatuh – Ash-Shaikh As'ad Muhammad Sa'eed As-Sagharji
3. Tadhkirah-tul-Muhadditheen – Ash-Shaikh Ghulam Rasool Saeedi

APPENDIX B

The Sources of Fiqh

The Holy Qur'an
The Holy Qur'an is the definite Word of Allah and He revealed it to the Holy Prophet Muhammad over a span of 23 years. It is the main source for finding answers to the issues in Fiqh because Allah commands in ayah 3 of Surah Al-A'raaf, **"Follow what has been sent down to you from your Lord."**

Sunnah of Rasoolullah based on Hadith (pl. Ahadith)
Anything said, done or (silently) approved by Rasoolullah is his sunnah. This is the second source for finding answers to Fiqh issues because The Holy Qur'an states, **"Whatever the Messenger gives you, take it, and whatever he prohibits you from, leave it."** [Surah Al-Hashr, ayah 7] It is used as a source on its own, and also in conjunction with the Holy Qur'an to explain it further.

Ijmaa
This means 'consensus', or 'the agreement of many scholars on any one issue'. If the answer to a problem cannot be found anywhere in the primary two sources (The Holy Qur'an and Sunnah), but is evident in the practice of many of the Blessed Companions or the scholars of the Ahl As-Sunnah agree on an answer collectively - then this is called Ijmaa. So the third source for Fiqh is ijmaa, because Rasoolullah said **"My Ummah will never (collectively) agree on misguidance"**.

Qiyaas
This means 'logical comparison' or 'analogy.' If the answer to a problem cannot be found anywhere in the first three sources, then it is up to a scholar- with the capability- to find a ruling based on his/her own judgement using previous cases and examples as a base. We are encouraged to use our intelligence by Allah Almighty in ayah 2 of Surah Al-Hashr, **"So think, oh you with insight."** The existence and acceptability of Qiyaas can also be proven through Hadith. For example when Rasoolullah sent Sayyiduna Mu'adh ibn Jabal as the governor of Yemen, he asked what he would use to pass just rulings and he answered, the Book of Allah, if I can't find the answer, then the example of the Messenger of Allah, if I don't find the answer there, then I shall use my intellect (he did not mention ijmaa because there was no ijmaa during the lifetime of Rasoolullah).

Note:
The third and fourth sources of Fiqh are not separate from the first two. Ijmaa and Qiyaas are only valid if they are taken from the Holy Qur'an and the Sunnah. Obviously no scholar makes up a ruling from his own thoughts, he will arrive at a definite answer based on his understanding of the two main sources. Anyone who rejects following any imam in fiqh should consider the evidence more carefully. If we claim that we follow The Holy Qur'an and Sunnah and take our rulings from it independently or directly, then we are contradicting ourselves by doing exactly what the imams did, except that they heard The Holy Qur'an and Ahadith directly from the Blessed Companions or the Taabi'een, so were in a much better situation to make these judgements than us.

GLOSSARY

Some General Fiqh Terms Regarding Tahaarah

Al-Hadath Al-Akbar (Major state of impurity): this state of impurity requires ghusl.

Al-Hadath Al-Asghar (Minor state of impurity): this state of impurity requires wudhu.

Dibaaghah (Tanning): the process of drying and colouring animal hide to make leather.

Ghair Makrooh (Not disliked): this refers to any action which is not disliked in the Shari'ah.

Ghair Mutahhir (Not purifying): this refers to a thing which does not purify, even though it may be pure in itself.

Ghaleezah (Extreme/heavy impurity): this is one of the types of najasah haqeeqiyyah and includes all those things which are considered very impure.

Ghusl: a ritual bath which is necessary to remove al-hadath al-akbar.

Hadath (Impurity): this means a state of impurity and it has two types. When the word hadath is used on its own, it usually means al-hadath al-asghar.

Haidh (Menstruation): this refers to a woman's monthly cycle which can last between 3 and 10 days.

Haqeeqiyyah (Najasah) (Physical impurity): this means physical najasah which can be seen and removed by washing.

Hukmiyyah (Najasah) (A state of impurity): this refers to the two states of hadath which cannot be seen but can be removed by wudhu or ghusl.

Istihaadhah (Continuous bleeding): this refers to blood which is discharged from within a woman's body through her private part.

Istinjaa: this is the word given to cleansing and washing the private parts after going to the toilet.

Janabah: A state of major impurity due to having sexual intercourse or releasing mani.

Junubi: A person in the state of janabah.

Khafeefah (Lesser/Light impurity): this is one of the two types of najasah haqeeqiyyah and includes all those things which are considered to be less impure.

Khuff (dual Khuffain): A leather (or waterproof) sock.

Kitaab At-Tahaarah (The Book of Purity): most books of Fiqh begin with the chapter on purity and the rulings associated with cleanliness.

Ma'zoor (Excused): A person who is excused from a ruling or command because of illness.

Makrooh (pl. Makroohaat): those actions which are disliked in the Shari'ah.

Mas'h (Wiping): this means using wet hands, or palms, and passing them over the required body part.

Mashkook (Doubted): this refers to all those things which are doubtful in their permissibility.

Maytah: this means any dead animal which has not been slaughtered according to the rules of the Shariah.

Muhdith: a person in the state of al-hadath al-asghar.

Musta'mal (Used): this refers to water which has been used for wudhu or ghusl.

Mustahaadhah: a woman in the state of istihaadhah.

Mutahhir (Purifying): this refers to all those things which are pure themselves and have the ability to purify other things too.

Najas (Impure): this refers to those things which are considered to be impure in the Shari'ah.

Najasah (pl. Anjaas): impurity.

Najasah Ghair-Mariyyah (Non-visible impurity): this refers to that impurity which is, or has become, invisible to the eye.

Najasah Mariyyah (Visible impurity): this refers to that impurity which is visible to the eye.

Nifaas (Postnatal bleeding): this refers to that bleeding which exits from a woman's private part after childbirth.

Niyyah (Intention): A firm objective in the heart before carrying out an action.

Nufasaa: a woman in the state of nifaas.

Qadhaa: making up for a missed fardh or wajib action.

Salah: the five daily prayers.

Soo-r (Leftover): this refers to water which another human or animal has drunk from and left behind.

Taahir (Pure): this refers to those things which are considered to be pure in the Shari'ah.

Tahaarah: Cleanliness or purity.

Tasmiyyah: to say the words of 'bismillah'.

Tayammum (Dry ablution): this refers to the wiping of the face and both arms with mutahhir earth with the intention of becoming purified.

Wudhu (Ablution): this refers to washing the face, arms and feet and wiping the head; it removes al-hadath al-asghar.

Some Extra Words Mentioned in This Book

Awrah: the parts of the body which must be covered.

Bukhari: Literally means anyone from Bukhara (a city in present day Uzbekistan). In the subject of hadith it refers, either to Imam Muhammad bin Ismail Al-Bukhari ؒ [194-256 AH], or "Sahih Bukhari" which is his authentic collection of ahadith and is one of the Sihaah Sittah (six authentic hadith collections).

Dirham: a silver coin used as currency in some Arab countries.

Du'a: supplication.

Fiqh: Literally means 'understanding,' and also refers to the branch of Islamic knowledge which involves understanding and taking rulings from the commands of Shari'ah.

Ghilaaf: a cover.

Hanafi: this means a person who follows the madh-hab of Imam A'dham Abu Hanifah Nu'man ibn Thaabit ؒ in fiqh.

Madh-hab (pl. Madhaahib): a school of thought or a way of practice in fiqh.

Mujallad: A type of khuff (sock) made entirely of leather.

Muna'all: A type of khuff which only has a leather sole and the rest is made of some other water-proof material.

Muqeem: a resident person.

Musaafir: a traveller.

Muslim: Literally means the one who accepts or submits and commonly used to mean any person belonging to the Islamic faith. When it is used as a reference for a hadith it refers to Imam Muslim bin Al-Hajjaaj ﷺ [206-261 AH] who was a great scholar of hadith and whose authentic collection of ahadith is recognised all over the world and is accepted unanimously as one of the six authentic books of hadith, the Sihaah Sittah.

Salah-tul-Eid: the prayer of 'Eid

Salah-tul-Janazah: the funeral prayer

Salah-tul-Jumu'ah: the Friday Congregational prayer

Shaf'i: Imam Muhammad bin Idrees Ash-Shaf'i ﷺ [150-204 AH] is the founder of one of the four schools of thought in fiqh. He was a great scholar of fiqh and hadith. He has a large following within the Ummah and his followrs are called Shaf'is.

Thawab: reward

'Uzr: an excuse

Sticker Section

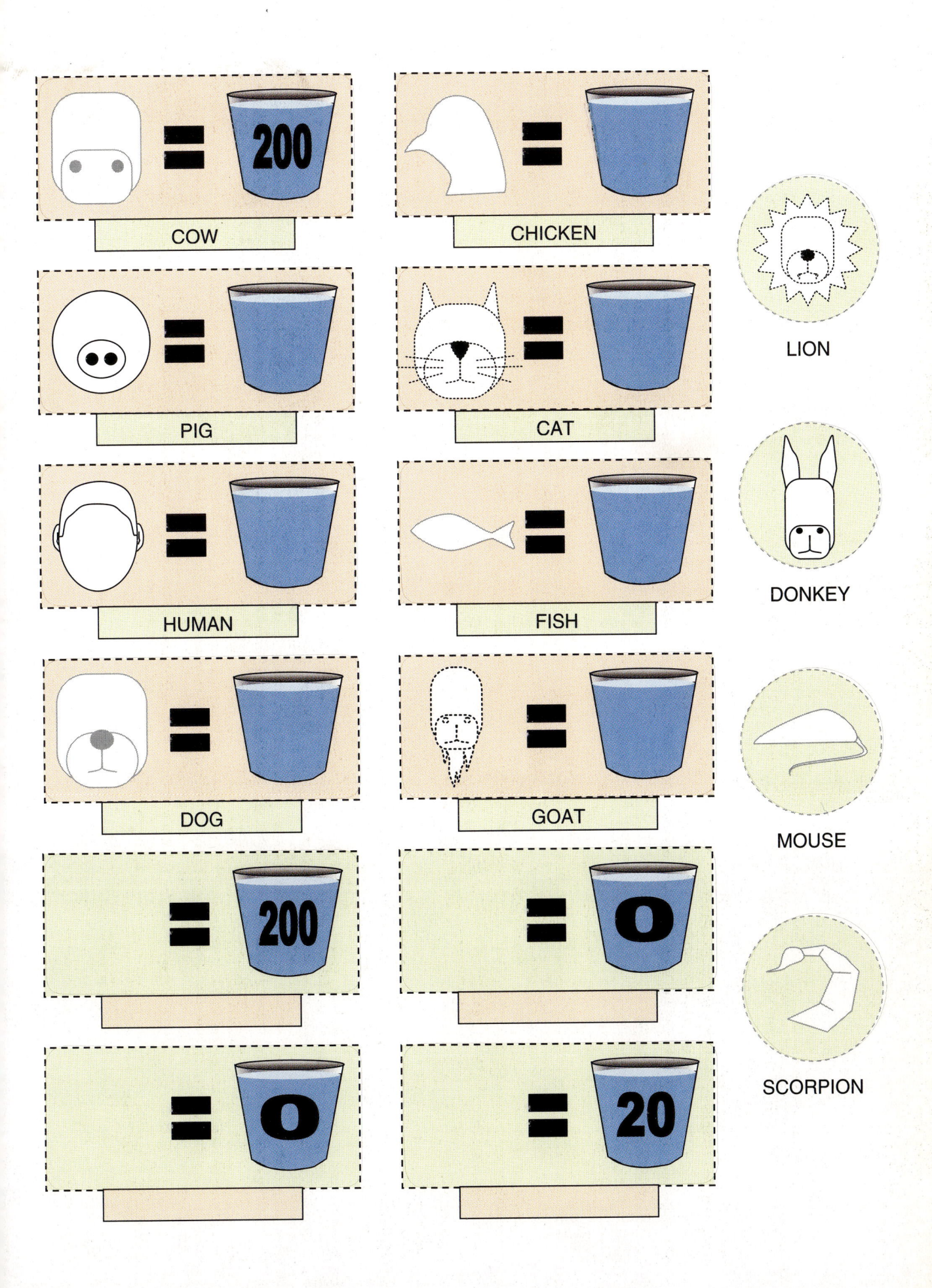

COW = 200	CHICKEN =
PIG =	CAT =
HUMAN =	FISH =
DOG =	GOAT =
= 200	= O
= O	= 20

LION

DONKEY

MOUSE

SCORPION

INSTRUCTIONS FOR ACTIVITY TWO

Here are the records that need to be filed. Peel each one off and sort out the ma'zoor patients from the non-ma'zoor ones. Now stick one record in each level of the correct filing cabinet taking care that the surnames are filed in alphabetical order.

Mrs S Hussain
Flu

Mr L Khan
Constant nosebleed

Mrs K Tabassum
Urine drops every 2-3 hours

Mr A Tahir
Non-stop wind

Miss Z Khatun
Infected wound, non-stop discharge of pus

Mr F Islam
Swollen ankles

Mr L Iqbal
Weak bladder - 1 urine drop every 5 minutes.

Mrs Y Alawiah
Consant bleeding (istihaadhah)

Ms N Ayn
Broken arm

Mr M Javed
Back pain

1 Peel off the picture and stick it in a green hexagon if it is pure or a red one if it is impure.

2 Explain why you have chosen to place this picture in this box.

MAYTAH COW'S SKIN BEFORE TANNING

Stick Picture Here

Stick Picture Here

PIG SKIN AFTER DIBAAGHAH

PIG SKIN BEFORE DIBAAGHAH

BONE

MAYTAH COW'S SKIN BEFORE TANNING

BONE & FAT

MAYTAH COW'S SKIN AFTER TANNING

TENDONS

FEATHERS

A PROPERLY SLAUGHTERED ZEBRA'S SKIN

LION MEAT

LION FUR

TUSKS

NOTES

NOTES

NOTES

NOTES

NOTES

NOTES

NOTES

ALSO BY STI PUBLISHING

العشرة الاخيرة
من سور القرآن الكريم

"The Last 10 Surahs of The Holy Qur'an"

150 Page Full-Colour Workbook.

£10.99

The blessing of Divine Speech is that whoever recites it as it should be recited is changed by it. 'The Last Ten' presents a lucid and insightful series of lessons bringing these Surahs alive in a creative and captivating manner, inspiring all ages to understand and comprehend the inner dimensions of these revelations. May all who take advantage of studying this excellent series be blessed with an ever increasing light of Imaan. And may all who have contributed to making this work a reality be honoured in both worlds, Ameen.

Uhkt Noor Al Madania
Madeenah Munawwarah 2009
http://almiskeenah.com

ALSO BY STI PUBLISHING

Tales from Dhikarville

WELCOME to Dhikarville!

...the town hosting the Brothers and Little Sisters each with an exciting and beneficial tale to tell.

Join them in their adventures as they learn important issues about the daily life of a Muslim.

Beware of Brother Sawm's mischief, look out for Little Sister Halaawah's party mishaps and much much more..!

Brother Da'wah
Brother Hadith
Brother Hajj
Brother 'Ilm
Brother Islaah
Brother Jumu'ah
Brother Khidmah
Brother Nasheed
Brother Sabr
Brother Salaam
Brother Salah
Brother Sawm
Brother Sidq
Brother Taqwaa
Brother Tasbeeh
Brother Tawheed
Bro. & L.S. Ramadan

Little Sister Birr
Little Sister Dua
Little Sister Halaawah
Little Sister Hidaayah
Little Sister Hijaab
Little Sister Hikmah
Little Sister Qira'ah
Little Sister Sadaqah
Little Sister Saeedah
Little Sister Salah
Little Sister Salaam
Little Sister Shukr
Little Sister Tahaarah
Little Sister Umrah
Little Sister Zakaah
Little Sister & Bro. Eid

KEEP AN EYE OUT for the latest books, posters, CDs and much more from Dhikarville!

Little Sister & Brother Series
Little Sister Salah
30 Page Story Book.

£2.00